Bread Machine Cookbook

Easy-to-Follow Guide to Baking Delicious Homemade Bread for Healthy Eating

Christopher Lester

Table of Contents

Table of Contents 3

Introduction 9

So, let's get started… 11

How to bake bread correctly in a bread maker? 14

How to make bread tastier and more useful? 15

Traditional Bread 17

All-Purpose White Bread 17

Mustard-Flavored General Bread 19

Faithful Italian Semolina Bread 21

Great British Muffin Bread 23

Sweet Molasses Wheat Bread 25

Honey-Flavored Bread 27

Crispy French Bread Delight 29

Toasty Paprika Bread 31

Delicious Italian Bread 33

Irish Beer Bread 35

Exuberant Egg Bread 37

Cool Pumpernickel Bread 39

Spicy Hawaiian Loaf 41

Herbed Sausage Bread 43

Ginger Bread & Oatmeal Medley 45

Spice & Herb Bread 47

Awesome Rosemary Bread 47

Original Italian Herb Bread 49

Lovely Aromatic Lavender Bread 51

Cinnamon & Dried Fruits Bread 53

Herbal Garlic Cream Cheese Delight 55

Oregano Mozza-Cheese Bread 57

Cumin Tossed Fancy Bread 59

Potato Rosemary Loaf 61

Delicious Honey Lavender Bread 63

Inspiring Cinnamon Bread 65

Energizing Anise Lemon Bread 67

Cinnamon-Flavored Raisin Bread 69

Turmeric Raisin Saffron Loaf 71

Fragrant Cardamom Bread 73

Grain, Seed & Nut Bread 75

Awesome Golden Corn Bread 75

Hearty Oatmeal Loaf 77

Cracked Wheat Bread 79

Orange Almond Loaf 81

Corn, Poppy Seeds & Sour Cream Bread 83

Simple Dark Rye Loaf 85

Pistachio Horseradish Apple Bread 87

Mesmerizing Walnut Bread 89

Bran Packed Healthy Bread 91

Orange Walnut Candied Loaf 93

Caramel Apple Pecan Loaf 95

Sesame Seeds & Onion Bread 97

Awesome Multigrain Bread 99

Delicious Rice Bread 101

Crunchy Wheat Herbed Bread 103

Sunflower Seeds & Oatmeal Bread 105

Delicious Flax Honey Loaf 107

Brazilian Nuts & Nutmeg Loaf 109

Multi-Purpose Seven Grain Bread 111

Cheese Bread 113

Ricotta & Chive Loaf 113

Double Cheese Overload 115

Cheddar Packed Olive Loaf 117

Cheesy Basil Loaf 119

Monterey Jack Loaf 121

Garlic & Parmesan Delight 122

Blue Cheese & Onion Loaf 124

Herb Garlic Cream Cheese Loaf 126

Moza Salami Loaf 128

Fruit Bread 130

Fruity French Bread 130

Succulent Cranberry Cinnamon Loaf 132

Wild Rice Cranberry Delight 134

Spice Pumpkin Bread 136

Lemon Flavored Poppy Loaf 138

Hearty Apple Pie Bread 140

Hawaiian Banana Bread 142

Hearty Cappuccino Orange Delight 144

Vegetable Bread 146

Healthy Celery Loaf 146

Cheesy Broccoli & Cauliflower Health Bread 148

Feisty Green Onion Bread 150

Hot Paprika Onion Bread	152
Caraway Potato Loaf	154
Zucchini Herbed Bread	156
Garden Variety Veggie Bread	158
Italian Onion Bread	160
Spicy Hot Red Pepper Loaf	162
Sauerkraut Rye Bread	164

Sweet Bread ... 166

Sweet Challah	166
Sweet Sour Maple Loaf	168
Sweet Almond Anise Bread	170
Choco Banana Oatmeal Loaf	172
Honeylicious Loaf	174
Healthy Sweet Flaxseed Loaf	176
Crunchy Sweet Raisin Loaf	178
Hazelnut Honey Loaf	180
Multi-Grain Honey Bread	182

Holiday Bread ... 184

Christmas Eggnog Bread	184
St. Patrick's Rum Bread	186

White Chocolate Cranberry Party Loaf 188

Portuguese Holiday Loaf 189

Grandma's Favorite Gingerbread 191

Kitchen Tools 193

    Kitchen Scale **193**

    Pastry Brush **194**

    Cheese Grater **194**

Cooking Measurement Conversion 195

Grocery Shopping List 196

From the Author 200

Our Recommendations 201

Recipe Index 202

Introduction

The day has come when you decide to finally bake bread in your bread machine.
There is no doubt you will have **the most delicious bread**. Just carefully read the instructions to your bread maker, and start with the easiest recipe.

Observe the information on the products that make up the bread (flour, liquid, butter, yeast, and other products). Make sure you already have them at home, and prepare them on the table in advance. Understand the units of measurement of the products needed to make this bread, and determine how you will measure them.

It should be remembered that in most bread makers, ingredients must be added to the form in a certain order. You must add them as described in the instructions to your bread maker. In most cases, liquid ingredients are poured first, then dry, and then yeast. With further instructions, you can bake a perfect loaf even your very first time. Common tips should work for all bread makers and are applicable in conjunction with instructions to your bread maker.

So, let's get started...

After you have selected the recipe for the bread you have chosen, prepare all the necessary products for the bread and determine how you will measure them.

Place the bread maker on a flat, fire-resistant surface, and make sure that it is away from heat sources (cooker or sunlight) and not in a draft. All these factors affect the temperature inside the bread maker.

1. Do not turn on the bread maker at this stage.

2. Open the cover.

3. Take the form by the handle, slightly turning it to the side or pulling up, depending on the model of your bread maker.

4. Pour in water (milk or other liquid, according to the recipe of your chosen bread). If the recipe contains an egg, it enters the weight of the liquid. For example, to bake bread weighing 750 grams and where you need 290-300 grams of liquid, you need to first put the egg in a measuring cup, and then add the liquid to reach 290-300 grams.

5. If your bread maker says that you first need to add dry ingredients, change the order of their loading in relation to our instructions.

6. Pour in the flour so that it completely covers the liquid. Salt, sugar, and oil should be put in at different angles so that they do not touch each other. Make a small "well" in the middle of the flour so that it does not reach the liquid, and add yeast to it. (If the yeast gets wet, it will start to work quickly).

7. Put the form in the bread maker.

8. Lower the knob and close the lid.

9. Then, plug the bread maker into an outlet.

10. Choose a program, the color of the crust, and the size of the loaf.

11. Press the START button.

12. Keep a wooden spatula ready; sometimes you have to scrape off the dry pieces of dough which stick at different stages of kneading.

13. When the dough is mixed, the bread maker will sound a beep, and you can add additional ingredients—for example, seeds or dried fruits. Open the lid, pour in, and close the lid. Do not be tempted to add more tasty additives to the dough than indicated in the recipe; this can cause the consistency of the dough to be broken.

14. At the end of the cycle, the bread maker will sound a beep to report that the bread is ready. Press the *STOP* button.

15. Turn off the bread maker.

16. Open the cover. To avoid getting burned, do not forget to put on oven mitts. Put the bread on a grate and let it cool. Cut the bread after it has completely cooled down. Many people wrap freshly baked bread in a clean kitchen towel and leave it for several hours; then it is cut better.

How to bake bread correctly in a bread maker?

- Be sure to **sift the flour** so that the bread turns tender and airy.

- **Liquid for bread** can be taken any of the following: water, yogurt, milk, sour cream, whey, buttermilk. They can be used by themselves or mixed in any proportions with water.
- Observe the **balance of flour and liquid** recommended for your bread maker model.

How to make bread tastier and more useful?

You can improve or slightly change the taste of bread by adding the following ingredients:

- If desired, **replace the vegetable oil** with cream to change the taste of bread to creamy.

- An **egg will improve the nutritional value** and flavor of bread (reduce the amount of water by the volume of the egg).

- **Sesame seed** will add piquancy.

- **Cottage cheese** will make the bread more elastic, and it will have a slight sourness.

- If you **add raisins, prunes, or dried apricots**, especially in grain bread, you will get an excellent balanced dietary product.

- **Bran** increases the content of vegetable fibers in bread.

- **Wheat germs** give the bread a nutty taste.

- **Spices**—for example, cinnamon or cardamom—make bread more fragrant.

- **Various oils** add flavor and softness to the bread.

- When **replacing water with milk**, the calorie content of bread rises.

Traditional Bread

All-Purpose White Bread

Yield: **1 pound loaf / 8 slices** | Prep Time + Cook Time: **2 - 3 hours**

Crust Type: **Medium** | Program: **Basic/White Bread**

¾ cup water at 80°F

1 tablespoon melted butter, cooled

1 tablespoon sugar

¾ teaspoon salt

2 tablespoons skim milk powder

2 cups white bread flour

¾ teaspoon instant yeast

DIRECTIONS:

1. Add all of the ingredients to your bread machine, carefully following the instructions of the manufacturer.
2. Set the program of your bread machine to *Basic/White Bread* and set crust type to *Medium*.
3. Press *START*.
4. Wait until the cycle completes.
5. Once the loaf is ready, take the bucket out and let the loaf cool for 5 minutes.
6. Gently shake the bucket to remove loaf.
7. Transfer to a cooling rack, slice, and serve.

NUTRITIONAL CONTENTS:

Total Carbs: 27g

Fiber: 2g

Protein: 44

Fat: 2g

Calories: 140

Mustard-Flavored General Bread

Yield: 2½ pound loaf / 20 slices | Prep Time + Cook Time: 2 - 3 hours

Crust Type: Medium Crust | Program: Basic/White Bread

- 1¼ cups milk
- 3 tablespoons sunflower milk
- 3 tablespoons sour cream
- 2 tablespoons dry mustard
- 1 whole egg, beaten
- ½ sachet sugar vanilla
- 4 cups flour
- 1 teaspoon dry yeast
- 2 tablespoons sugar
- 2 teaspoon salt

DIRECTIONS:

1. Take out the bread maker's bucket and pour in milk and sunflower oil; stir and then add sour cream and beaten egg.
2. Add flour, salt, sugar, mustard powder, vanilla sugar, and mix well.
3. Make a small groove in the flour and sprinkle yeast.
4. Transfer the bucket to your bread maker and cover.
5. Set the program of your bread machine to *Basic/White Bread* and set crust type to *Medium*.
6. Press *START*.
7. Wait until the cycle completes.
8. Once the loaf is ready, take the bucket out and let the loaf cool for 5 minutes.
9. Gently shake the bucket to remove loaf.
10. Transfer to a cooling rack, slice, and serve.

NUTRITIONAL CONTENTS:

Total Carbs: 54g

Fiber: 1g

Protein: 10g

Fat: 10g

Calories: 340

Faithful Italian Semolina Bread

Yield: 1½ pound loaf / 8 slices | Prep Time + Cook Time: 3½ hours

Crust Type: Medium | Program: Sandwich Mode/Italian Mode

- 1 cup water
- 1 teaspoon salt
- 2½ tablespoons butter
- 2½ teaspoons sugar
- 2¼ cups flour
- ⅓ cups semolina
- 1½ teaspoons dry yeast

DIRECTIONS:

1. Add all of the ingredients to your bread machine, carefully following the instructions of the manufacturer.
2. Set the program of your bread machine to *Italian Bread/Sandwich* mode and set crust type to *Medium*.
3. Press *START*.
4. Wait until the cycle completes.
5. Once the loaf is ready, take the bucket out and let the loaf cool for 5 minutes.
6. Gently shake the bucket to remove loaf.
7. Transfer to a cooling rack, slice, and serve.

NUTRITIONAL CONTENTS:

Total Carbs: 45g

Fiber: 1g

Protein: 7g

Fat: 10g

Calories: 302

Great British Muffin Bread

Yield: 1 pound loaf / 8 slices | Prep Time + Cook Time: 2 - 3 hours

Crust Type: Medium | Program: Basic/White Bread

⅔ cup buttermilk at 80°F

1 tablespoon melted butter, cooled

1 tablespoon sugar

¾ teaspoon salt

¼ teaspoon baking powder

1¾ cups white bread flour

1⅛ teaspoons instant yeast

DIRECTIONS:

1. Add all of the ingredients to your bread machine, carefully following the instructions of the manufacturer.
2. Set the program of your bread machine to *Basic/White Bread* and set crust type to *Medium*.
3. Press *START*.
4. Wait until the cycle completes.
5. Once the loaf is ready, take the bucket out and let the loaf cool for 5 minutes.
6. Gently shake the bucket to remove loaf.
7. Transfer to a cooling rack, slice, and serve.

NUTRITIONAL CONTENTS:

Total Carbs: 24g

Fiber: 2g

Protein: 4g

Fat: 2g

Calories: 131

Sweet Molasses Wheat Bread

Yield: 1 pound loaf / 8 slices | Prep Time + Cook Time: 2 - 3 hours

Crust Type: Medium | Program: Basic/White Bread

½ cup water at 80°F

¼ cup milk at 80°F

2 teaspoons melted butter, cooled

2 tablespoons honey

1 tablespoon molasses

1 teaspoon sugar

1 tablespoon skim milk powder

½ teaspoon salt

1 teaspoon unsweetened cocoa powder

1¼ cups whole wheat flour

1 cup white bread flour

1 teaspoon instant yeast

DIRECTIONS:

1. Add all of the ingredients to your bread machine, carefully following the instructions of the manufacturer.
2. Set the program of your bread machine to *Basic/White Bread* and set crust type to *Medium*.
3. Press *START*.
4. Wait until the cycle completes.
5. Once the loaf is ready, take the bucket out and let the loaf cool for 5 minutes.
6. Gently shake the bucket to remove loaf.
7. Transfer to a cooling rack, slice, and serve.

NUTRITIONAL CONTENTS:

Total Carbs: 34g

Fiber: 2g

Protein: 4

Fat: 2g

Calories: 164

Honey-Flavored Bread

Yield: 1½ pound loaf / 8 slices | Prep Time + Cook Time: 3½ hours

Crust Type: Medium | Program: Basic/White Bread

- 2¼ cups white flour
- ¼ cup rye flour
- 1 cup water
- 1 whole egg, beaten
- 1 tablespoon vegetable oil
- 1 teaspoon salt
- 1½ tablespoons honey
- 1 teaspoon dry yeast

DIRECTIONS:

1. Add all of the ingredients to your bread machine, carefully following the instructions of the manufacturer.
2. Set the program of your bread machine to *Basic/White Bread* and set crust type to *Medium*.
3. Press *START*.
4. Wait until the cycle completes.
5. Once the loaf is ready, take the bucket out and let the loaf cool for 5 minutes.
6. Gently shake the bucket to remove loaf.
7. Transfer to a cooling rack, slice, and serve.

NUTRITIONAL CONTENTS:

Total Carbs: 33g

Fiber: 1g

Protein: 6g

Fat: 3g

Calories: 177

Crispy French Bread Delight

Yield: **1 pound loaf / 8 slices** | Prep Time + Cook Time: **3 - 3½ hours**

Crust Type: Light | Program: French Bread

⅔ cup water at 80°F

2 teaspoons olive oil

1 tablespoon sugar

⅔ teaspoon salt

2 cups white bread flour

1 teaspoon instant yeast

DIRECTIONS:

1. Add all of the ingredients to your bread machine, carefully following the instructions of the manufacturer.
2. Set the program of your bread machine to *French Bread* and set crust type to *Light*.
3. Press *START*.
4. Wait until the cycle completes.
5. Once the loaf is ready, take the bucket out and let the loaf cool for 5 minutes.
6. Gently shake the bucket to remove loaf.
7. Transfer to a cooling rack, slice, and serve.

NUTRITIONAL CONTENTS:

Total Carbs: 26g

Fiber: 1g

Protein: 3g

Fat: 2g

Calories: 135

Toasty Paprika Bread

Yield: 1½ pound loaf / 10 slices | Prep Time + Cook Time: 2 - 3 hours

Crust Type: Light | Program: Basic/White Bread

- 1½ teaspoons yeast
- 3 cups wheat flour
- 2 tablespoons sugar
- 1 teaspoon salt
- 1½ tablespoons butter
- 1 cup water
- 2 teaspoons paprika (depending on your desired spice level)
- 1 cup dried tomatoes

DIRECTIONS:

1. Add all of the ingredients to your bread machine, carefully following the instructions of the manufacturer.
2. Set the program of your bread machine to *Basic/White Bread* and set crust type to *Light*.
3. Press START.
4. Wait until the cycle completes.
5. Once the loaf is ready, take the bucket out and let the loaf cool for 5 minutes.
6. Gently shake the bucket to remove loaf.
7. Transfer to a cooling rack, slice, and serve.

NUTRITIONAL CONTENTS:

Total Carbs: 40g

Fiber: 2g

Protein: 6g

Fat: 3g

Calories: 203

Delicious Italian Bread

Yield: 1 pound loaf / 8 slices | Prep Time + Cook Time: 2 - 3 hours

Crust Type: Medium | Program: Basic/White Bread

⅔ cup water at 80°F

1 tablespoon olive oil

1 tablespoon sugar

¾ teaspoon salt

2 cups white bread flour

1 teaspoon instant yeast

DIRECTIONS:

1. Add all of the ingredients to your bread machine, carefully following the instructions of the manufacturer.
2. Set the program of your bread machine to *Basic/White Bread* and set crust type to *Medium*.
3. Press START.
4. Wait until the cycle completes.
5. Once the loaf is ready, take the bucket out and let the loaf cool for 5 minutes.
6. Gently shake the bucket to remove loaf.
7. Transfer to a cooling rack, slice, and serve.

NUTRITIONAL CONTENTS:

Total Carbs: 26g

Fiber: 1g

Protein: 3g

Fat: 2g

Calories: 136

Irish Beer Bread

Yield: 1½ pound loaf / 14 slices | Prep Time + Cook Time: 3 hours 20 minutes

Crust Type: Medium | Program: Basic/White Bread

1⅙ cups light beer

2 tablespoons liquid honey

1 tablespoon olive oil

1 teaspoon salt

1 teaspoon cumin

2¾ cups wheat flour

1½ teaspoons dry yeast

DIRECTIONS:

1. Pour the beer into a tall glass, and then into another tall glass. Keep repeating the process several times in order to release carbon dioxide.
2. Add all of the ingredients to your bread machine, carefully following the instructions of the manufacturer.
3. Set the program of your bread machine to *Basic/White Bread* and set crust type to *Medium*.
4. Press *START*.
5. Wait until the cycle completes.
6. Once the loaf is ready, take the bucket out and let the loaf cool for 5 minutes.
7. Gently shake the bucket to remove loaf.
8. Transfer to a cooling rack, slice, and serve.

NUTRITIONAL CONTENTS:

Total Carbs: 38g

Fiber: 1g

Protein: 5

Fat: 2g

Calories: 201

Exuberant Egg Bread

Yield: 1 pound loaf / 8 slices | Prep Time + Cook Time: 3 - 3½ hours

Crust Type: Light | Program: French Bread

½ cup + 2 tablespoons milk at 80° F

2⅔ tablespoons melted butter, cooled

1 whole egg, beaten

2⅔ tablespoons sugar

1 teaspoon salt

2 cups white bread flour

¾ teaspoon instant yeast

DIRECTIONS:

1. Add all of the ingredients to your bread machine, carefully following the instructions of the manufacturer.
2. Set the program of your bread machine to *French Bread* and set crust type to *Light*.
3. Press *START*.
4. Wait until the cycle completes.
5. Once the loaf is ready, take the bucket out and let the loaf cool for 5 minutes.
6. Gently shake the bucket to remove loaf.
7. Transfer to a cooling rack, slice, and serve.

NUTRITIONAL CONTENTS:

Total Carbs: 29g

Fiber: 1g

Protein: 5g

Fat: 5g

Calories: 184

Cool Pumpernickel Bread

Yield: 1 pound loaf / 8 slices | Prep Time + Cook Time: 2 - 3 hours

Crust Type: Light | Program: Basic/White Bread

½ cup water at 80°F

¼ cup brewed coffee at 80°F

2 tablespoons dark molasses

5 teaspoons sugar

4 teaspoons melted butter, cooled

1 tablespoon powdered skim milk

1 teaspoon salt

4 teaspoons unsweetened cocoa powder

⅔ cup dark rye flour

½ cup whole wheat bread flour

1 teaspoon caraway seeds

1 cup white bread flour

1½ teaspoons active dry yeast

DIRECTIONS:

1. Add all of the ingredients to your bread machine, carefully following the instructions of the manufacturer.
2. Set the program of your bread machine to *Basic/White Bread* and set crust type to *Light*.
3. Press *START*.
4. Wait until the cycle completes.
5. Once the loaf is ready, take the bucket out and let the loaf cool for 5 minutes.
6. Gently shake the bucket to remove loaf.
7. Transfer to a cooling rack, slice, and serve.

NUTRITIONAL CONTENTS:

Total Carbs: 33g

Fiber: 1g

Protein: 5g

Fat: 3g

Calories: 168

Spicy Hawaiian Loaf

Yield: 1 pound loaf / 8 slices | Prep Time + Cook Time: 3 hours 10 minutes

Crust Type: Light | Program: Dough Bread

- 1¼ cups milk
- 1 tablespoon vanilla extract
- ¼ cup brown sugar
- 2 tablespoons granulated sugar
- 1¼ teaspoon salt
- ¼ teaspoon ground coriander
- 1/8 teaspoon ground cardamom
- 2 tablespoons butter, melted
- 3½ cups bread flour
- 1 pack rapid rise yeast

DIRECTIONS:

1. Add all of the ingredients to your bread machine, carefully following the instructions of the manufacturer.
2. Set the program of your bread machine to *Dough Bread* and set crust type to *Light*.
3. Press START.
4. Wait until the cycle completes.
5. Turn the dough out onto a floured surface and punch it down to form a loaf.
6. Pre-heat your oven to 350°F.
7. Grease 9x5 inch bread pan and place the dough in.
8. Cover and let it rise for 25-35 minutes.
9. Transfer to oven and bake for 35-45 minutes until golden brown.
10. Remove loaf and let it cool.
11. Transfer to a cooling rack, slice and serve.
12. Enjoy!

NUTRITIONAL CONTENTS:

Total Carbs: 7g

Fiber: 1g

Protein: 1g

Fat: 3g

Calories: 57

Herbed Sausage Bread

Yield: 1 pound loaf / 8 slices | Prep Time + Cook Time: 3 hours 10 minutes

Crust Type: Medium | Program: Basic/White Bread

- 2/3 cup water at room temperature
- 1 tablespoon olive oil
- 1 tablespoon sugar
- ¾ teaspoon salt
- ¼ teaspoon dried basil
- ¼ teaspoon dried oregano
- 1/ cup cooked chopped Italian sausage
- 2 cups white bread flour
- 1 teaspoon bread machine yeast

DIRECTIONS:

1. Add all of the ingredients to your bread machine, carefully following the instructions of the manufacturer.
2. Set the program of your bread machine to *Basic/White Bread* and set crust type to *Medium*.
3. Press START.
4. Wait until the cycle completes.
5. Once the loaf is ready, take the bucket out and let the loaf cool for 5 minutes.
6. Gently shake the bucket to remove loaf.
7. Transfer to a cooling rack, slice and serve.
8. Enjoy!

NUTRITIONAL CONTENTS:

Total Carbs: 26g

Fiber: 1g

Protein: 4g

Fat: 3g

Calories: 143

Ginger Bread & Oatmeal Medley

Yield: 1 pound loaf / 8 slices | Prep Time + Cook Time: 2 - 3 hours

Crust Type: Medium | Program: Basic/White Bread

- 1 cup + 1 tablespoon water at room temperature
- ½ cup molasses
- 1 tablespoon canola oil
- 3 cups old-fashioned oats
- 1½ teaspoons ground cinnamon
- 1 to 1½ teaspoons ground ginger
- 1 teaspoon salt
- ½ teaspoon orange peel, grated
- ¼ teaspoon ground nutmeg
- ¼ teaspoon ground cloves
- 1 pack active dry yeast

DIRECTIONS:

1. Add all of the ingredients to your bread machine, carefully following the instructions of the manufacturer.
2. Set the program of your bread machine to *Basic/White Bread* and set crust type to *Medium*.
3. Press START.
4. Wait until the cycle completes.
5. Once the loaf is ready, take the bucket out and let the loaf cool for 5 minutes.
6. Gently shake the bucket to remove loaf.
7. Transfer to a cooling rack, slice and serve.
8. Enjoy!

NUTRITIONAL CONTENTS:

Total Carbs: 27g

Fiber: 1g

Protein: 4g

Fat: 1g

Calories: 131

Spice & Herb Bread

Awesome Rosemary Bread

Yield: 1 pound loaf / 8 slices | Prep Time + Cook Time: 2 - 3 hours

Crust Type: Medium | Program: Basic/White Bread

¾ cup + 1 tablespoon water at 80°F

1⅔ tablespoons melted butter, cooled

2 teaspoons sugar

1 teaspoon salt

1 tablespoon fresh rosemary, chopped

2 cups white bread flour

1⅓ teaspoons instant yeast

DIRECTIONS:

1. Add all of the ingredients to your bread machine, carefully following the instructions of the manufacturer.
2. Set the program of your bread machine to *Basic/White Bread* and set crust type to *Medium*.
3. Press *START*.
4. Wait until the cycle completes.
5. Once the loaf is ready, take the bucket out and let the loaf cool for 5 minutes.
6. Gently shake the bucket to remove loaf.
7. Transfer to a cooling rack, slice, and serve.

NUTRITIONAL CONTENTS:

Total Carbs: 25g

Fiber: 1g

Protein: 4g

Fat: 3g

Calories: 142

Original Italian Herb Bread

Yield: 2½ pound loaf / 20 slices | Prep Time + Cook Time: 3½ hours

Crust Type: Medium | Program: French

1 cup water at 80°F

½ cup olive brine

1½ tablespoons butter

3 tablespoons sugar

2 teaspoons salt

5⅓ cups flour

2 teaspoons yeast

20 olives, black/green

1½ teaspoons Italian herbs

DIRECTIONS:

1. Cut olives into slices.
2. Add all of the ingredients to your bread machine (except olives), carefully following the instructions of the manufacturer.
3. Set the program of your bread machine to *French Bread* and set crust type to *Medium*.
4. Press *START*.
5. Once the maker beeps, add olives.
6. Wait until the cycle completes.
7. Once the loaf is ready, take the bucket out and let the loaf cool for 5 minutes.
8. Gently shake the bucket to remove loaf.
9. Transfer to a cooling rack, slice, and serve.

NUTRITIONAL CONTENTS:

Total Carbs: 71g

Fiber: 1g

Protein: 10g

Fat: 7g

Calories: 386

Lovely Aromatic Lavender Bread

Yield: 1 pound loaf / 8 slices | Prep Time + Cook Time: 2 - 3 hours

Crust Type: Medium | Program: Basic/White Bread

¾ cup milk at 80°F

1 tablespoon melted butter, cooled

1 tablespoon sugar

¾ teaspoon salt

1 teaspoon fresh lavender flower, chopped

¼ teaspoon lemon zest

¼ teaspoon fresh thyme, chopped

2 cups white bread flour

¾ teaspoon instant yeast

DIRECTIONS:

1. Add all of the ingredients to your bread machine, carefully following the instructions of the manufacturer.
2. Set the program of your bread machine to *Basic/White Bread* and set crust type to *Medium*.
3. Press *START*.
4. Wait until the cycle completes.
5. Once the loaf is ready, take the bucket out and let the loaf cool for 5 minutes.
6. Gently shake the bucket to remove loaf.
7. Transfer to a cooling rack, slice, and serve.

NUTRITIONAL CONTENTS:

Total Carbs: 27g
Fiber: 1g
Protein: 4g
Fat: 2g
Calories: 144

Cinnamon & Dried Fruits Bread

Yield: 2 pound loaf / 16 slices | Prep Time + Cook Time: 3½ hours

Crust Type: Medium | Program: Basic/White Bread

- 2¾ cups flour
- 1½ cups dried fruits
- 4 tablespoons sugar
- 2½ tablespoons butter
- 1 tablespoon milk powder
- 1 teaspoon cinnamon
- ½ teaspoon ground nutmeg
- ¼ teaspoon vanillin
- ½ cup peanuts
- powdered sugar, for sprinkling
- 1 teaspoon salt

DIRECTIONS:

1. Add all of the ingredients to your bread machine (except peanuts and powdered sugar), carefully following the instructions of the manufacturer.
2. Set the program of your bread machine to *Basic/White Bread* and set crust type to *Medium*.
3. Press *START*.
4. Once the bread maker signals, moisten dough with a bit of water and add peanuts.
5. Wait until the cycle completes.
6. Once the loaf is ready, take the bucket out and let the loaf cool for 5 minutes.
7. Gently shake the bucket to remove loaf.
8. Sprinkle with powdered sugar.
9. Transfer to a cooling rack, slice, and serve.

NUTRITIONAL CONTENTS:

Total Carbs: 65g

Fiber: 1g

Protein: 5g

Fat: 4g

Calories: 315

Herbal Garlic Cream Cheese Delight

Yield: 1 pound loaf / 8 slices | Prep Time + Cook Time: 2 - 3 hours

Crust Type: Medium | Program: Basic/White Bread

- ⅓ cup water at 80°F
- ⅓ cup herb and garlic cream cheese mix, at room temp
- 1 whole egg, beaten, at room temp
- 4 teaspoons melted butter, cooled
- 1 tablespoon sugar
- ⅔ teaspoon salt
- 2 cups white bread flour
- 1 teaspoon instant yeast

DIRECTIONS:

1. Add all of the ingredients to your bread machine, carefully following the instructions of the manufacturer.
2. Set the program of your bread machine to *Basic/White Bread* and set crust type to *Medium*.
3. Press *START*.
4. Wait until the cycle completes.
5. Once the loaf is ready, take the bucket out and let the loaf cool for 5 minutes.
6. Gently shake the bucket to remove loaf.
7. Transfer to a cooling rack, slice, and serve.

NUTRITIONAL CONTENTS:

Total Carbs: 27g

Fiber: 2g

Protein: 5g

Fat: 6g

Calories: 182

Oregano Mozza-Cheese Bread

Yield: 2 pound loaf / 16 slices | Prep Time + Cook Time: 3½ hours

Crust Type: Dark | Program: Basic/White Bread

1 cup (milk + egg) mixture

½ cup mozzarella cheese

2¼ cups flour

¾ cup whole grain flour

2 tablespoons sugar

1 teaspoon salt

2 teaspoons oregano

1½ teaspoons dry yeast

DIRECTIONS:

1. Add all of the ingredients to your bread machine, carefully following the instructions of the manufacturer.
2. Set the program of your bread machine to *Basic/White Bread* and set crust type to *Dark*.
3. Press *START*.
4. Wait until the cycle completes.
5. Once the loaf is ready, take the bucket out and let the loaf cool for 5 minutes.
6. Gently shake the bucket to remove loaf.
7. Transfer to a cooling rack, slice, and serve.

NUTRITIONAL CONTENTS:

Total Carbs: 40g

Fiber: 1g

Protein: 7.7g

Fat: 2.1g

Calories: 209

Cumin Tossed Fancy Bread

Yield: 2 pound loaf / 16 slices | Prep Time + Cook Time: 3½ hours

Crust Type: Medium | Program: French Bread

5⅓ cups flour

1½ teaspoons salt

1½ tablespoons sugar

1 tablespoon dry yeast

1¾ cups water

2 tablespoons cumin

3 tablespoons sunflower oil

DIRECTIONS:

1. Add warm water to the bread machine bucket.
2. Add salt, sugar, and sunflower oil.
3. Sift in wheat flour and add yeast.
4. Set the program of your bread machine to *French Bread* and set crust type to *Medium*.
5. Press *START*.
6. Once the maker beeps, add cumin.
7. Wait until the cycle completes.
8. Once the loaf is ready, take the bucket out and let the loaf cool for 5 minutes.
9. Gently shake the bucket to remove loaf.
10. Transfer to a cooling rack, slice, and serve.

NUTRITIONAL CONTENTS:

Total Carbs: 67g

Fiber: 2g

Protein: 9.5g

Fat: 7g

Calories: 368

Potato Rosemary Loaf

Yield: 2½ pound loaf / 20 slices | Prep Time + Cook Time: 3½ hours

Crust Type: Medium | Program: Bread With Filling

- 4 cups wheat flour
- 1 tablespoon sugar
- 1 tablespoon sunflower oil
- 1½ teaspoons salt
- 1½ cups water
- 1 teaspoon dry yeast
- 1 cup mashed potatoes, ground through a sieve
- crushed rosemary to taste

DIRECTIONS:

1. Add flour, salt, and sugar to the bread maker bucket and attach mixing paddle.
2. Add sunflower oil and water.
3. Put in yeast as directed.
4. Set the program of your bread machine to *Bread With Filling* mode and set crust type to *Medium*.
5. Press *START*.
6. Once the bread maker beeps and signals to add more ingredients, open lid and add mashed potatoes and chopped rosemary.
7. Wait until the cycle completes.
8. Once the loaf is ready, take the bucket out and let the loaf cool for 5 minutes.
9. Gently shake the bucket to remove loaf.
10. Transfer to a cooling rack, slice, and serve.

NUTRITIONAL CONTENTS:

Total Carbs: 54g

Fiber: 1g

Protein: 8g

Fat: 3g

Calories: 276

Delicious Honey Lavender Bread

Yield: 2 pound loaf / 16 slices | Prep Time + Cook Time: 3½ hours

Crust Type: Medium | Program: Basic/White Bread

- 1½ cups wheat flour
- 2⅓ cups wholemeal flour
- 1 teaspoon fresh yeast
- 1½ cups water
- 1 teaspoon lavender
- 1½ tablespoons honey
- 1 teaspoon salt

DIRECTIONS:

1. Sift both types of flour in a bowl and mix.
2. Add all of the ingredients to your bread machine, carefully following the instructions of the manufacturer.
3. Set the program of your bread machine to *Basic/White Bread* and set crust type to *Medium*.
4. Press *START*.
5. Wait until the cycle completes.
6. Once the loaf is ready, take the bucket out and let the loaf cool for 5 minutes.
7. Gently shake the bucket to remove loaf.
8. Transfer to a cooling rack, slice, and serve.

NUTRITIONAL CONTENTS:

Total Carbs: 46g

Fiber: 1g

Protein: 7.5g

Fat: 1.5g

Calories: 226

Inspiring Cinnamon Bread

Yield: 1 pound loaf / 8 slices | Prep Time + Cook Time: 2 - 3 hours

Crust Type: Medium | Program: Basic/White Bread

⅔ cup milk at 80°F

1 whole egg, beaten

3 tablespoons melted butter, cooled

⅓ cup sugar

⅓ teaspoon salt

1 teaspoon ground cinnamon

2 cups white bread flour

1⅓ teaspoons active dry yeast

DIRECTIONS:

1. Add all of the ingredients to your bread machine, carefully following the instructions of the manufacturer.
2. Set the program of your bread machine to *Basic/White Bread* and set crust type to *Medium*.
3. Press *START*.
4. Wait until the cycle completes.
5. Once the loaf is ready, take the bucket out and let the loaf cool for 5 minutes.
6. Gently shake the bucket to remove loaf.
7. Transfer to a cooling rack, slice, and serve.

NUTRITIONAL CONTENTS:

Total Carbs: 34g

Fiber: 1g

Protein: 5g

Fat: 5g

Calories: 198

Energizing Anise Lemon Bread

Yield: 1 pound loaf / 8 slices | Prep Time + Cook Time: 2 - 3 hours

Crust Type: Medium | Program: Basic/White Bread

⅔ cup water at 80°F

1 whole egg, at room temperature

2⅔ tablespoons butter, melted and cooled

2⅔ tablespoons honey

⅓ teaspoon salt

⅔ teaspoon anise seed

⅔ teaspoon lemon zest

2 cups white bread flour

1⅓ teaspoons instant yeast

DIRECTIONS:

1. Add all of the ingredients to your bread machine, carefully following the instructions of the manufacturer.
2. Set the program of your bread machine to *Basic/White Bread* and set crust type to *Medium*.
3. Press *START*.
4. Wait until the cycle completes.
5. Once the loaf is ready, take the bucket out and let the loaf cool for 5 minutes.
6. Gently shake the bucket to remove loaf.
7. Transfer to a cooling rack, slice, and serve.

NUTRITIONAL CONTENTS:

Total Carbs: 34g

Fiber: 1g

Protein: 5g

Fat: 5g

Calories: 198

Cinnamon-Flavored Raisin Bread

Yield: 1 pound loaf / 8 slices | Prep Time + Cook Time: 3 - 3½ hours

Crust Type: Medium | Program: Sweet Bread

¾ cup milk at 80°F
1 tablespoon melted butter, cooled
1 tablespoon sugar
¾ teaspoon salt

½ teaspoon ground cinnamon
2 cups white bread flour
1 teaspoon instant yeast
½ cup golden raisins

DIRECTIONS:

1. Add all of the ingredients to your bread machine (except raisins), carefully following the instructions of the manufacturer.
2. Set the program of your bread machine to *Sweet Bread* and set crust type to *Medium*.
3. Press *START*.
4. Wait until the cycle completes.
5. Add raisins at the raisin/nut signal (should be after 1 - 1½ hours).
6. Once the loaf is ready, take the bucket out and let the loaf cool for 5 minutes.
7. Gently shake the bucket to remove loaf.
8. Transfer to a cooling rack, slice, and serve.

NUTRITIONAL CONTENTS:

Total Carbs: 34g

Fiber: 2g

Protein: 4g

Fat: 3g

Calories: 173

Turmeric Raisin Saffron Loaf

Yield: 2½ pound loaf / 20 slices | Prep Time + Cook Time: 3½ hours

Crust Type: Dark | Program: Basic/White Bread

1½ cups milk at 80°F

2 tablespoons sugar

1½ teaspoons salt

¼ teaspoon powdered saffron + turmeric

2 tablespoons butter

1 tablespoon vanilla sugar

4½ cups flour

1 teaspoon yeast

1 cup raisins

DIRECTIONS:

1. Add all of the ingredients to your bread machine (except raisins), carefully following the instructions of the manufacturer.
2. Set the program of your bread machine to *Basic/White Bread* and set crust type to *Medium*.
3. Press *START*.
4. Once the bread maker gives the signal for adding more ingredients, add raisins.
5. Wait until the cycle completes.
6. Once the loaf is ready, take the bucket out and let the loaf cool for 5 minutes.
7. Gently shake the bucket to remove loaf.
8. Transfer to a cooling rack, slice, and serve.

NUTRITIONAL CONTENTS:

Total Carbs: 74g

Fiber: 2g

Protein: 9.6g

Fat: 2.6g

Calories: 378

Fragrant Cardamom Bread

Yield: 1 pound loaf / 8 slices | Prep Time + Cook Time: 2 - 3 hours

Crust Type: Medium | Program: Basic/White Bread

½ cup milk at 80°F

1 egg, at room temperature

1 teaspoon melted butter, cooled

4 teaspoons honey

⅔ teaspoon salt

⅔ teaspoon ground cardamom

2 cups white bread flour

¾ teaspoon instant yeast

DIRECTIONS:

1. Add all of the ingredients to your bread machine, carefully following the instructions of the manufacturer.
2. Set the program of your bread machine to *Basic/White Bread* and set crust type to *Medium*.
3. Press *START*.
4. Wait until the cycle completes.
5. Once the loaf is ready, take the bucket out and let the loaf cool for 5 minutes.
6. Gently shake the bucket to remove loaf.
7. Transfer to a cooling rack, slice, and serve.

NUTRITIONAL CONTENTS:

Total Carbs: 29g

Fiber: 2g

Protein: 5g

Fat: 2g

Calories: 149

Grain, Seed & Nut Bread

Awesome Golden Corn Bread

Yield: 1 - 2 pound loaf / 12 - 16 slices | Prep Time + Cook Time: 1½ - 2 hours

Crust Type: Medium | Program: Quick/Rapid Bread Mode

1 cup buttermilk at 80°F

2 whole eggs, at room temperature

¼ cup melted butter, cooled

1⅓ cups all-purpose flour

1 cup cornmeal

¼ cup sugar

1 tablespoon baking powder

1 teaspoon salt

DIRECTIONS:

1. Add buttermilk, butter, and eggs to your bread machine, carefully following the manufacturer instructions.
2. Program the machine for *Quick/Rapid Bread* mode and press *START*.
3. While the wet ingredients are being mixed in the machine, take a small bowl and stir in flour, cornmeal, sugar, baking powder, and salt.
4. After the first fast mix is done and the machine gives the signal, add dry ingredients.
5. Wait until the whole cycle completes.
6. Once the loaf is done, take the bucket out and let it cool for 5 minutes.
7. Gently shake the basket to remove the loaf and transfer to a cooling rack.
8. Slice and serve!

NUTRITIONAL CONTENTS:

Total Carbs: 24g
Fiber: 2g
Protein: 4g
Fat: 5g
Calories: 158

Hearty Oatmeal Loaf

Yield: 1 pound loaf / 8 slices | Prep Time + Cook Time: 2 - 3 hours

Crust Type: Medium | Program: Basic/White Bread

¾ cup water at 80°F

2 tablespoons melted butter, cooled

2 tablespoons sugar

1 teaspoon salt

¾ cup quick oats

1½ cups white bread flour

1 teaspoon instant yeast

DIRECTIONS:

1. Add all of the ingredients to your bread machine, carefully following the instructions of the manufacturer.
2. Set the program of your bread machine to *Basic/White Bread* and set crust type to *Medium*.
3. Press *START*.
4. Wait until the cycle completes.
5. Once the loaf is ready, take the bucket out and let the loaf cool for 5 minutes.
6. Gently shake the bucket to remove loaf.
7. Transfer to a cooling rack, slice, and serve.

NUTRITIONAL CONTENTS:

Total Carbs: 26g

Fiber: 1g

Protein: 4g

Fat: 4g

Calories: 149

Cracked Wheat Bread

Yield: 1 pound loaf / 8 slices | Prep Time + Cook Time: 2 - 3 hours

Crust Type: Medium | Program: Basic/White Bread

3 tablespoons cracked wheat

¾ cup + 2 tablespoons boiling water

2⅔ tablespoons melted butter, cooled

1 teaspoon salt

2 tablespoons honey

⅔ cup whole wheat flour

1⅓ cups white bread flour

1⅓ teaspoons instant yeast

DIRECTIONS:

1. Take the bucket of your bread machine and add cracked wheat and water; let it sit for 30 minutes until liquid is 80°F.
2. Add rest of the ingredients to your bread machine, carefully following the instructions of the manufacturer.
3. Set the program of your bread machine to *Basic/White Bread* and set crust type to *Medium*.
4. Press *START*.
5. Wait until the cycle completes.
6. Once the loaf is ready, take the bucket out and let the loaf cool for 5 minutes.
7. Gently shake the bucket to remove loaf.
8. Transfer to a cooling rack, slice, and serve.

NUTRITIONAL CONTENTS:

Total Carbs: 31g

Fiber: 1g

Protein: 4g

Fat: 4g

Calories: 176

Orange Almond Loaf

Yield: 2 pound loaf / 16 slices | Prep Time + Cook Time: 3½ hours

Crust Type: Medium | Program: Basic/White Bread

4 cups flour

¾ cup sweet almonds, chopped

3 tablespoons brown sugar

peels of 2 oranges, grated

1 cup orange juice

2 tablespoons sweet almond oil

1 teaspoon salt

powdered sugar for sprinkling

DIRECTIONS:

1. Add all of the ingredients to your bread machine (except the powdered sugar and ¼ cup of almonds), carefully following the instructions of the manufacturer.
2. Set the program of your bread machine to *Basic/White Bread* and set crust type to *Medium*.
3. Press *START*.
4. Wait until the cycle completes.
5. Once the loaf is ready, take the bucket out and let the loaf cool for 5 minutes.
6. Gently shake the bucket to remove loaf.
7. Moisten the surface with water and sprinkle with remaining almonds and powdered sugar.
8. Transfer to a cooling rack, slice, and serve.

NUTRITIONAL CONTENTS:

Total Carbs: 61.1g

Fiber: 1g

Protein: 8.5g

Fat: 7g

Calories: 347

Corn, Poppy Seeds & Sour Cream Bread

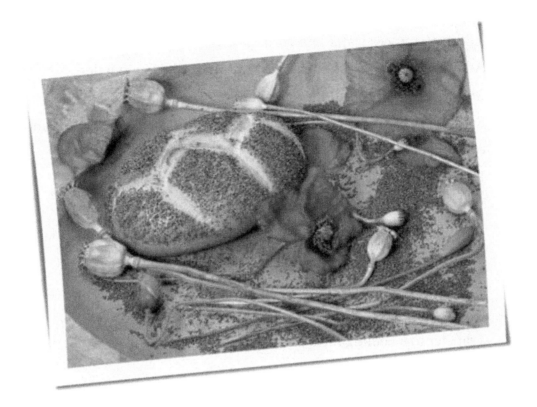

Yield: 2 pound loaf / 16 slices | Prep Time + Cook Time: 3½ hours

Crust Type: Medium | Program: Basic/White Bread

3½ cups wheat flour

1¾ cups corn flour

5 ounces sour cream

2 tablespoons corn oil

2 teaspoons dried yeast

2 teaspoons salt

16 ¼ ounces water

poppy seeds for sprinkling

DIRECTIONS:

1. Add 16¼ ounces water and corn oil to the bread maker bucket.
2. Add flour, sour cream, sugar, and salt from different angles.
3. Make a groove in the flour and add yeast.
4. Set the program of your bread machine to *Basic/White Bread* and set crust type to *Medium*.
5. Press *START*.
6. Wait until the cycle completes.
7. Once the loaf is ready, take the bucket out and let the loaf cool for 5 minutes.
8. Gently shake the bucket to remove loaf.
9. Moisten the surface with water and sprinkle with poppy seeds.
10. Transfer to a cooling rack, slice, and serve.

NUTRITIONAL CONTENTS:

Total Carbs: 64g

Fiber: 1g

Protein: 9g

Fat: 10g

Calories: 374

Simple Dark Rye Loaf

Yield: 1 pound loaf / 8 slices | Prep Time + Cook Time: 2 - 3 hours

Crust Type: Medium | Program: Basic/White Bread

⅔ cup water at 80°F

1 tablespoon melted butter, cooled

¼ cup molasses

¼ teaspoon salt

1 tablespoon unsweetened cocoa powder

½ cup rye flour

pinch of ground nutmeg

1¼ cups white bread flour

1⅛ teaspoons instant yeast

DIRECTIONS:

1. Add all of the ingredients to your bread machine, carefully following the instructions of the manufacturer.
2. Set the program of your bread machine to *Basic/White Bread* and set crust type to *Medium*.
3. Press *START*.
4. Wait until the cycle completes.
5. Once the loaf is ready, take the bucket out and let the loaf cool for 5 minutes.
6. Gently shake the bucket to remove loaf.
7. Transfer to a cooling rack, slice, and serve.

NUTRITIONAL CONTENTS:

Total Carbs: 29g

Fiber: 1g

Protein: 4g

Fat: 2g

Calories: 144

Pistachio Horseradish Apple Bread

Yield: 2 pound loaf / 16 slices | Prep Time + Cook Time: 2 - 3 hours

Crust Type: Medium | Program: Basic/White Bread

- 3 cups wheat flour
- 2 whole eggs, beaten
- 3 tablespoons horseradish, grated
- ½ cup apple puree
- 1 tablespoon sugar
- 4 tablespoons olive oil
- ½ cup pistachios, peeled and chopped
- 1 teaspoon dried yeast
- 1 cup + 1 tablespoon water
- 1 teaspoon salt

DIRECTIONS:

1. Lightly beat eggs in a bowl.
2. Add 1 cup + 1 tablespoons water to bread maker bucket.
3. Add olive oil.
4. Add flour, applesauce, half of the pistachios, horseradish, and eggs into the bucket.
5. Mix well and make a small groove in the middle.
6. Add yeast.
7. Add salt and sugar to the bucket from different sides.
8. Set the program of your bread machine to *Basic/White Bread* and set crust type to *Medium*.
9. Press *START*.
10. Wait until the cycle completes.
11. Once the loaf is ready, take the bucket out and let the loaf cool for 5 minutes.
12. Gently shake the bucket to remove loaf.
13. Transfer to a cooling rack, slice, and serve.

NUTRITIONAL CONTENTS:

Total Carbs: 41g

Fiber: 2g

Protein: 8g

Fat: 10g

Calories: 291

Mesmerizing Walnut Bread

Yield: 2 pound loaf / 12 - 16 slices | Prep Time + Cook Time: 3 - 4 hours

Crust Type: Light | Program: French

4 cups wheat flour

½ cup water

½ cup milk

2 whole eggs, beaten

½ cup walnut

1 tablespoon vegetable oil

1 tablespoon sugar

1 teaspoon salt

1 teaspoon yeast

DIRECTIONS:

1. Add milk, water, vegetable oil, and eggs to the bread maker bucket.
2. Pour in sifted wheat flour.
3. Add salt, sugar, and yeast on three sides of the bucket.
4. Set the program of your bread machine to *French Bread* and set crust type to *Light*.
5. Press *START*.
6. Let the kneading begin and close the lid.
7. Slightly fry the walnuts in a dry frying pan until crispy; then let them cool.
8. Once the bread maker gives the signal, add the nuts to the bread maker.
9. Mix with a spatula.
10. Let the remaining cycle complete.
11. Once the loaf is ready, take the bucket out and let the loaf cool for 5 minutes.
12. Gently shake the bucket to remove loaf.
13. Transfer to a cooling rack, slice, and serve.

NUTRITIONAL CONTENTS:

Total Carbs: 40g
Fiber: 1g
Protein: 9g
Fat: 7g
Calories: 257

Bran Packed Healthy Bread

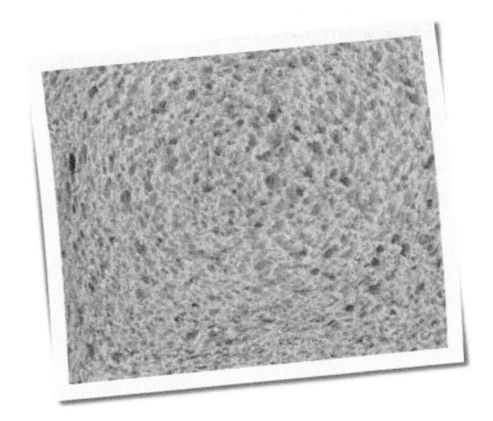

Yield: 1 pound loaf / 8 slices | Prep Time + Cook Time: 2 - 3 hours

Crust Type: Light | Program: Basic/White Bread

¾ cup milk at 80°F
1½ tablespoons melted butter, cooled
2 tablespoons sugar
1 teaspoon salt
¼ cup wheat bran
1¾ cups white bread flour
1 teaspoon instant yeast

DIRECTIONS:

1. Add all of the ingredients to your bread machine, carefully following the instructions of the manufacturer.
2. Set the program of your bread machine to *Basic/White Bread* and set crust type to *Light*.
3. Press *START*.
4. Wait until the cycle completes.
5. Once the loaf is ready, take the bucket out and let the loaf cool for 5 minutes.
6. Gently shake the bucket to remove loaf.
7. Transfer to a cooling rack, slice, and serve.

NUTRITIONAL CONTENTS:

Total Carbs: 26g

Fiber: 1g

Protein: 4g

Fat: 4g

Calories: 149

Orange Walnut Candied Loaf

Yield: 1½ pound loaf / 12 slices | Prep Time + Cook Time: 24 hours

Crust Type: Medium | Program: Basic/White/Sweet Bread

- ½ cup warm whey
- 1 tablespoon yeast
- 4 tablespoons sugar
- 2 orange juice
- 4 cups flour
- 1 teaspoon salt
- 1½ tablespoons salt
- 3 teaspoons orange zest
- ⅓ teaspoon vanilla
- 3 tablespoons (walnut + almonds)
- ½ cup candied fruit

DIRECTIONS:

1. Add all of the ingredients to your bread machine, carefully following the instructions of the manufacturer.
2. Set the program of your bread machine to *Basic/White Bread* and set crust type to *Medium*.
3. Press *START*.
4. Wait until the cycle completes.
5. Once the loaf is ready, take the bucket out and let the loaf cool for 5 minutes.
6. Gently shake the bucket to remove loaf.
7. Transfer to a cooling rack, slice, and serve.

NUTRITIONAL CONTENTS:

Total Carbs: 82g

Fiber: 1g

Protein: 12g

Fat: 7g

Calories: 437

Caramel Apple Pecan Loaf

Yield: 1 pound loaf / 8 slices | Prep Time + Cook Time: 3 hours 50 minutes

Crust Type: Medium | Program: Basic/White Bread

- 1 cup water
- 2 tablespoons butter
- 3 cups bread flour
- ¼ cup packed brown sugar
- ¾ teaspoon ground cinnamon
- 1 teaspoon salt
- 2 teaspoons quick yeast
- ½ cup apple, chopped
- ⅓ cup coarsely chopped pecans, toasted

DIRECTIONS:

1. Add all of the ingredients to your bread machine (except apples and pecans), carefully following the instructions of the manufacturer.
2. Set the program of your bread machine to *Basic/White Bread* and set crust type to *Medium*.
3. Press *START*.
4. Once the bread maker beeps, add pecans and apples.
5. Wait until the cycle completes.
6. Once the loaf is ready, take the bucket out and let the loaf cool for 5 minutes.
7. Gently shake the bucket to remove loaf.
8. Transfer to a cooling rack, slice, and serve.

NUTRITIONAL CONTENTS:

Total Carbs: 32g

Fiber: 2g

Protein: 4g

Fat: 5g

Calories: 185

Sesame Seeds & Onion Bread

Yield: 2½ pound loaf / 20 slices | Prep Time + Cook Time: 2 - 3 hours

Crust Type: Medium | Program: Basic/White Bread

- ¾ cup water
- 3⅔ cups flour
- ¾ cup cottage cheese
- 2 tablespoons soft butter
- 2 tablespoons sugar
- 1½ teaspoons salt
- 1½ tablespoons sesame seeds
- 2 tablespoons dried onion
- 1¼ teaspoons dry yeast

DIRECTIONS:

1. Add all of the ingredients to your bread machine, carefully following the instructions of the manufacturer.
2. Set the program of your bread machine to *Basic/White Bread* and set crust type to *Medium*.
3. Press *START*.
4. Wait until the cycle completes.
5. Once the loaf is ready, take the bucket out and let the loaf cool for 5 minutes.
6. Gently shake the bucket to remove loaf.
7. Transfer to a cooling rack, slice, and serve.

NUTRITIONAL CONTENTS:

Total Carbs: 48g

Fiber: 2g

Protein: 10g

Fat: 5g

Calories: 277

Awesome Multigrain Bread

Yield: 1 pound loaf / 8 slices | Prep Time + Cook Time: 2 - 3 hours

Crust Type: Medium | Program: Basic/White Bread

¾ cup water at 80°F

1 tablespoon melted butter

½ tablespoon honey

½ teaspoon salt

¾ cup multigrain flour

1⅓ cups white bread flour

1 teaspoon active dry yeast

DIRECTIONS:

1. Add all of the ingredients to your bread machine, carefully following the instructions of the manufacturer.
2. Set the program of your bread machine to *Basic/White Bread* and set crust type to *Medium*.
3. Press *START*.
4. Wait until the cycle completes.
5. Once the loaf is ready, take the bucket out and let the loaf cool for 5 minutes.
6. Gently shake the bucket to remove loaf.
7. Transfer to a cooling rack, slice, and serve.

NUTRITIONAL CONTENTS:

Total Carbs: 27g

Fiber: 2g

Protein: 4g

Fat: 2g

Calories: 145

Delicious Rice Bread

Yield: 2 pound loaf / 16 slices | Prep Time + Cook Time: 3½ hours

Crust Type: Medium | Program: Basic/White Bread

4½ cups wheat flour

1 cup rice, cooked

1 whole egg, beaten

2 tablespoons milk powder

2 teaspoons dried yeast

2 tablespoons butter

1 tablespoon sugar

2 teaspoon salt

1 ¼ cups water

DIRECTIONS:

1. Add 1¼ cups of water to the bread maker bucket.
2. Add beaten egg.
3. Add flour, rice, and milk powder.
4. Add butter, sugar, and salt in different corners of the bucket.
5. Make a groove in the middle of the flour and add yeast.
6. Set the program of your bread machine to *Basic/White Bread* and set crust type to *Medium*.
7. Press *START*.
8. Wait until the cycle completes.
9. Once the loaf is ready, take the bucket out and let the loaf cool for 5 minutes.
10. Gently shake the bucket to remove loaf.
11. Transfer to a cooling rack, slice, and serve.

NUTRITIONAL CONTENTS:

Total Carbs: 61g
Fiber: 1g
Protein: 9g
Fat: 5g
Calories: 328

Crunchy Wheat Herbed Bread

Yield: 1 pound loaf / 8 slices | Prep Time + Cook Time: 3 hours 40 minutes

Crust Type: Medium | Program: Basic/White Bread

- 1¼ cups water
- 1½ cups bread flour
- 1½ cups whole wheat flour
- 2 tablespoons sugar
- 2 tablespoons dry milk
- 2 tablespoons butter
- 1½ teaspoons salt
- 1½ teaspoons dried basil leaves
- 1 teaspoon dried thyme leaves
- 2 teaspoons bread machine yeast
- ½ cup dry roasted sunflower nuts

DIRECTIONS:

1. Add all of the ingredients to your bread machine, carefully following the instructions of the manufacturer (except nuts).
2. Set the program of your bread machine to *Basic/White Bread* and set crust type to *Medium*.
3. Press START.
4. Add nuts once the machine beeps.
5. Wait until the cycle completes.
6. Once the loaf is ready, take the bucket out and let the loaf cool for 5 minutes.
7. Gently shake the bucket to remove loaf.
8. Transfer to a cooling rack, slice and serve.
9. Enjoy!

NUTRITIONAL CONTENTS:

Total Carbs: 28g

Fiber: 1g

Protein: 6g

Fat: 5g

Calories: 170

Sunflower Seeds & Oatmeal Bread

Yield: 1 pound loaf / 8 slices | Prep Time + Cook Time: 3 - 4 hours

Crust Type: Light | Program: Basic/White Bread

- 1 cup water
- ¼ cup honey
- 2 tablespoons butter
- 3 cups bread flour
- ½ cup quick-cooking oats
- 2 tablespoons dry milk
- 1¼ teaspoons salt
- 2¼ teaspoons bread machine yeast
- ½ cup sunflower nuts

DIRECTIONS:

1. Add all of the ingredients to your bread machine, carefully following the instructions of the manufacturer (except nuts.)
2. Set the program of your bread machine to *Basic/White Bread* and set crust type to *Light*.
3. Press START.
4. Once the machine beeps, add nuts.
5. Wait until the cycle completes.
6. Once the loaf is ready, take the bucket out and let the loaf cool for 5 minutes.
7. Gently shake the bucket to remove loaf.
8. Transfer to a cooling rack, slice and serve.
9. Enjoy!

NUTRITIONAL CONTENTS:

Total Carbs: 36g

Fiber: 1g

Protein: 6g

Fat: 5g

Calories: 200

Delicious Flax Honey Loaf

Yield: 1 pound loaf / 8 slices | Prep Time + Cook Time: 2 - 3 hours

Crust Type: Medium | Program: Basic/White Bread

¾ cup milk, at room temperature

1 tablespoon melted butter

1 tablespoon honey

¾ teaspoon salt

2 tablespoons flaxseeds

2 cups white bread flour

¾ teaspoon bread machine yeast

DIRECTIONS:

1. Add all of the ingredients to your bread machine, carefully following the instructions of the manufacturer.
2. Set the program of your bread machine to *Basic/White Bread* and set crust type to *Medium*.
3. Press START.
4. Wait until the cycle completes.
5. Once the loaf is ready, take the bucket out and let the loaf cool for 5 minutes.
6. Gently shake the bucket to remove loaf.
7. Transfer to a cooling rack, slice and serve.
8. Enjoy!

NUTRITIONAL CONTENTS:

Total Carbs: 28g

Fiber: 1g

Protein: 6g

Fat: 3g

Calories: 158

Brazilian Nuts & Nutmeg Loaf

Yield: 1 pound loaf / 8 slices | Prep Time + Cook Time: 2 - 3 hours

Crust Type: Medium | Program: Basic/White Bread

1¼ cups water

2 tablespoons oil

3 cups wholemeal bread flour

1½ teaspoons salt

1 teaspoon fresh grated nutmeg

1½ teaspoons instant active dried yeast

¾ cup brazil nuts, coarsely chopped

DIRECTIONS:

1. Add all of the ingredients to your bread machine, carefully following the instructions of the manufacturer (except nuts).
2. Set the program of your bread machine to *Basic/White Bread* and set crust type to *Medium*.
3. Press START.
4. Add nuts once the machine beeps,
5. Wait until the cycle completes.
6. Once the loaf is ready, take the bucket out and let the loaf cool for 5 minutes.
7. Gently shake the bucket to remove loaf.
8. Transfer to a cooling rack, slice and serve.
9. Enjoy!

NUTRITIONAL CONTENTS:

Total Carbs: 8g
Fiber: 1g
Protein: 3g
Fat: 7g
Calories: 98

Multi-Purpose Seven Grain Bread

Yield: 1 pound loaf / 8 slices | Prep Time + Cook Time: 2 - 3 hours

Crust Type: Medium | Program: Basic/White Bread

- 1 1/3 cups warm water
- 1 tablespoon active dry yeast
- 3 tablespoons dry milk powder
- 2 tablespoons honey
- 2 teaspoons salt
- 1 whole egg
- 1 cup whole wheat flour
- 2½ cups bread flour
- ¾ cups 7-grain cereal

DIRECTIONS:

1. Add all of the ingredients to your bread machine, carefully following the instructions of the manufacturer.
2. Set the program of your bread machine to *Basic/White* Bread and set crust type to *Medium*.
3. Press START.
4. Wait until the cycle completes.
5. Once the loaf is ready, take the bucket out and let the loaf cool for 5 minutes.
6. Gently shake the bucket to remove loaf.
7. Transfer to a cooling rack, slice and serve.
8. Enjoy!

NUTRITIONAL CONTENTS:

Total Carbs: 50g

Fiber: 1g

Protein: 10g

Fat: 6g

Calories: 47

Cheese Bread

Ricotta & Chive Loaf

Yield: 1 pound loaf / 8 slices | Prep Time + Cook Time: 3 hours 10 minutes

Crust Type: Light | Program: Basic/White Bread

1 cup lukewarm water

1/3 cup whole ricotta cheese

1½ teaspoons salt

1 tablespoon granulated sugar

3 cups bread flour

½ cup chopped chives

2½ teaspoons instant yeast

DIRECTIONS:

1. Add all of the ingredients to your bread machine, carefully following the instructions of the manufacturer (except dried fruits).
2. Set the program of your bread machine to *Basic/White Bread* and set crust type to *Light*.
3. Press START.
4. Once the machine beeps, add fruits.
5. Wait until the cycle completes.
6. Once the loaf is ready, take the bucket out and let the loaf cool for 5 minutes.
7. Gently shake the bucket to remove loaf.
8. Transfer to a cooling rack, slice and serve.
9. Enjoy!

NUTRITIONAL CONTENTS:

Total Carbs: 17g, Fiber: 1g, Protein: 3g, Fat: 0g, Calories: 92

Double Cheese Overload

Yield: 1 pound loaf / 8 slices | Prep Time + Cook Time: 3 hours 10 minutes

Crust Type: Light | Program: Basic/White Bread

¾ cup + 1 tablespoons milk at 80°F

2 teaspoons butter, melted and cooled

4 teaspoons sugar

2/3 teaspoon salt

1/3 teaspoon fresh ground pepper

Pinch of cayenne pepper

1 cup (4 ounces) shredded aged sharp cheddar cheese

1/3 cup shredded/grated parmesan cheese

2 cups white bread flour

¾ teaspoon instant yeast

DIRECTIONS:

1. Add all of the ingredients to your bread machine, carefully following the instructions of the manufacturer.
2. Set the program of your bread machine to *Basic/White Bread* and set crust type to *Light*.
3. Press START.
4. Wait until the cycle completes.
5. Once the loaf is ready, take the bucket out and let the loaf cool for 5 minutes.
6. Gently shake the bucket to remove loaf.
7. Transfer to a cooling rack, slice and serve.
8. Enjoy!

NUTRITIONAL CONTENTS:

Total Carbs: 28g

Fiber: 1g

Protein: 9g

Fat: 4g

Calories: 183

Cheddar Packed Olive Loaf

Yield: 1 pound loaf / 8 slices | Prep Time + Cook Time: 3 hours 10 minutes

Crust Type: Light | Program: Basic/White Bread

1 cup water at room temperature

4 teaspoons sugar

¾ teaspoon salt

1¼ cups shredded sharp cheddar cheese

3 cups bread flour

2 teaspoons active dry yeast

¾ cup pimiento olives, drained and sliced

DIRECTIONS:

1. Add all of the ingredients to your bread machine, carefully following the instructions of the manufacturer (except olives).
2. Set the program of your bread machine to *Basic/White Bread* and set crust type to *Light*.
3. Press START.
4. Once the machine beeps, add olives.
5. Wait until the cycle completes.
6. Once the loaf is ready, take the bucket out and let the loaf cool for 5 minutes.
7. Gently shake the bucket to remove loaf.
8. Transfer to a cooling rack, slice and serve.
9. Enjoy!

NUTRITIONAL CONTENTS:

Total Carbs: 19g

Fiber: 1g

Protein: 5g

Fat: 4g

Calories: 124

Cheesy Basil Loaf

Yield: 1 pound loaf / 8 slices | Prep Time + Cook Time: 3 hours 10 minutes

Crust Type: Light | Program: Basic/White Bread

2/3 cup milk, at 80°F

2 teaspoons melted butter, cooled

2 teaspoons sugar

2/3 teaspoon dried basil

½ cup (2 ounces) shredded sharp cheddar cheese

½ teaspoon salt

2 cups white bread flour

1 teaspoon active dry yeast

DIRECTIONS:

1. Add all of the ingredients to your bread machine, carefully following the instructions of the manufacturer.
2. Set the program of your bread machine to *Basic/White Bread* and set crust type to *Light*.
3. Press START.
4. Wait until the cycle completes.
5. Once the loaf is ready, take the bucket out and let the loaf cool for 5 minutes.
6. Gently shake the bucket to remove loaf.
7. Transfer to a cooling rack, slice and serve.
8. Enjoy!

NUTRITIONAL CONTENTS:

Total Carbs: 26g

Fiber: 1g

Protein: 6g

Fat: 4g

Calories: 166

Monterey Jack Loaf

Yield: 1 pound loaf / 8 slices | Prep Time + Cook Time: 2 - 3 hours
Crust Type: Medium | Program: Basic/White Bread

1 cup warm water
1 teaspoon salt
2 tablespoons white sugar
½ cup Monterey Jack cheese, shredded
6 tablespoons fresh jalapeno pepper, chopped
3 cups bread flour
½ teaspoon active dry yeast

DIRECTIONS:

1. Add all of the ingredients to your bread machine, carefully following the instructions of the manufacturer.
2. Set the program of your bread machine to *Basic/White Bread* and set crust type to *Medium*.
3. Press START.
4. Wait until the cycle completes.
5. Once the loaf is ready, take the bucket out and let the loaf cool for 5 minutes.
6. Gently shake the bucket to remove loaf.
7. Transfer to a cooling rack, slice and serve.

NUTRITIONAL CONTENTS:

Total Carbs: 27g, Fiber: 1g, Protein: 5g, Fat: 2g, Calories: 152

Garlic & Parmesan Delight

Yield: 1 pound loaf / 8 slices | Prep Time + Cook Time: 2 - 3 hours

Crust Type: Medium | Program: Basic/White Bread

1 cup water at room temperature

2 tablespoons + 1½ teaspoon butter, soft

1 tablespoon honey

2/3 cup parmesan cheese, grated

1½ teaspoon garlic powder

¾ teaspoon salt

3 cups bread flour

2¼ teaspoon dry yeast (active)

DIRECTIONS:

1. Add all of the ingredients to your bread machine, carefully following the instructions of the manufacturer.
2. Set the program of your bread machine to *Basic/White Bread* and set crust type to *Medium*.
3. Press START.
4. Wait until the cycle completes.
5. Once the loaf is ready, take the bucket out and let the loaf cool for 5 minutes.
6. Gently shake the bucket to remove loaf.
7. Transfer to a cooling rack, slice and serve.
8. Enjoy!

NUTRITIONAL CONTENTS:

Total Carbs: 18g

Fiber: 1g

Protein: 5g

Fat: 3g

Calories: 112

Blue Cheese & Onion Loaf

Yield: 1 pound loaf / 8 slices | Prep Time + Cook Time: 3 hours 10 minutes

Crust Type: Light | Program: Basic/White Bread

- ¾ cup + 1 tablespoon water at 80°F
- 1 whole egg
- 2 teaspoons melted butter, cooled
- 3 tablespoons powdered skim milk
- 2 teaspoons sugar
- ½ teaspoon salt
- 1/3 cup crumbled blue cheese
- 2 teaspoons dried onion flakes
- 2 cups white bread flour
- 3 tablespoons instantly mashed potato flakes
- ¾ teaspoons bread machine/ active dry yeast

DIRECTIONS:

1. Add all of the ingredients to your bread machine, carefully following the instructions of the manufacturer.
2. Set the program of your bread machine to *Basic/White Bread* and set crust type to *Light*.
3. Press START.
4. Wait until the cycle completes.
5. Once the loaf is ready, take the bucket out and let the loaf cool for 5 minutes.
6. Gently shake the bucket to remove loaf.
7. Transfer to a cooling rack, slice and serve.
8. Enjoy!

NUTRITIONAL CONTENTS:

Total Carbs: 27g

Fiber: 1g

Protein: 6g

Fat: 3g

Calories: 164

Herb Garlic Cream Cheese Loaf

Yield: 1 pound loaf / 8 slices | Prep Time + Cook Time: 3 - 4 hours

Crust Type: Light | Program: Basic/White Bread

1/3 cup water, at room temperature

1/3 cup herb and garlic cream cheese mixture

1 teaspoon bread machine yeast

1 whole egg

4 teaspoons melted butter, cooled

1 tablespoon sugar

2/3 teaspoon salt

2 cups white bread flour

DIRECTIONS:

1. Add all of the ingredients to your bread machine, carefully following the instructions of the manufacturer.
2. Set the program of your bread machine to *Basic/White Bread* and set crust type to *Light*.
3. Press START.
4. Wait until the cycle completes.
5. Once the loaf is ready, take the bucket out and let the loaf cool for 5 minutes.
6. Gently shake the bucket to remove loaf.
7. Transfer to a cooling rack, slice and serve.
8. Enjoy!

NUTRITIONAL CONTENTS:

Total Carbs: 27g

Fiber: 1g

Protein: 5g

Fat: 6g

Calories: 182

Moza Salami Loaf

Yield: 1 pound loaf / 8 slices | Prep Time + Cook Time: 3 hours 10 minutes

Crust Type: Light | Program: Basic/White Bread

- ¾ cup water, at 80°F
- 1/3 cup shredded mozzarella cheese
- 4 teaspoons sugar
- 2/3 teaspoon salt
- 2/3 teaspoon dried basil
- Pinch of garlic powder
- 2 cups + 2 tablespoons white bread flour
- 1 teaspoon bread machine/ instant yeast
- ½ cup finely diced hot salami

DIRECTIONS:

1. Add all of the ingredients to your bread machine, carefully following the instructions of the manufacturer (except salami).
2. Set the program of your bread machine to *Basic/White Bread* and set crust type to *Light*.
3. Press START.
4. Add salami once the machine signals.
5. Wait until the cycle completes.
6. Once the loaf is ready, take the bucket out and let the loaf cool for 5 minutes.
7. Gently shake the bucket to remove loaf.
8. Transfer to a cooling rack, slice and serve.
9. Enjoy!

NUTRITIONAL CONTENTS:

Total Carbs: 28g

Fiber: 1g

Protein: 6g

Fat: 3g

Calories: 164

Fruit Bread

Fruity French Bread

Yield: 1 pound loaf / 8 slices | Prep Time + Cook Time: 1 - 2 hours

Crust Type: Light | Program: Basic/White Bread

¾ cup canned pears, mashed
¼ cup water
1 tablespoon honey
1 egg, slightly beaten

3 cups bread flour
1/8 teaspoon pepper
1 teaspoon dry yeast

DIRECTIONS:

1. Add all of the ingredients to your bread machine, carefully following the instructions of the manufacturer.
2. Set the program of your bread machine to *Basic/White Bread* and set crust type to *Light*.
3. Press START.
4. Wait until the cycle completes.
5. Once the loaf is ready, take the bucket out and let the loaf cool for 5 minutes.
6. Gently shake the bucket to remove loaf.
7. Transfer to a cooling rack, slice and serve.
8. Enjoy!

NUTRITIONAL CONTENTS:

Total Carbs: 9g, Fiber: 2g, Protein: 5g, Fat: 9g, Calories: 158

Succulent Cranberry Cinnamon Loaf

Yield: 1 pound loaf / 8 slices | Prep Time + Cook Time: 3 hours 10 minutes

Crust Type: Light | Program: Basic/White Bread

- 1¼ cup water
- 2 tablespoons soft butter
- 2½ tablespoons sugar
- 3½ cups bread flour
- 2 ¼ teaspoons dry yeast
- 1 cup dried cranberries
- 1½ teaspoons cinnamon

DIRECTIONS:

1. Add all of the ingredients (except cranberries) to your bread machine, carefully following the instructions of the manufacturer.
2. Set the program of your bread machine to *Basic/White Bread* and set crust type to *Light*.
3. Press START.
4. Once the bread maker signals, add cranberries.
5. Wait until the cycle completes.
6. Once the loaf is ready, take the bucket out and let the loaf cool for 5 minutes.
7. Gently shake the bucket to remove loaf.
8. Transfer to a cooling rack, slice and serve.
9. Enjoy!

NUTRITIONAL CONTENTS:

Total Carbs: 37g

Fiber: 1g

Protein: 4.1g

Fat: 1.3g

Calories: 167

Wild Rice Cranberry Delight

Yield: 1 pound loaf / 8 slices | Prep Time + Cook Time: 3 hours 10 minutes

Crust Type: Light | Program: Basic/White Bread

1¼ cups water

¼ cup skim milk powder

1¼ teaspoon salt

2 tablespoons liquid honey

1 tablespoon extra-virgin olive oil

3 cups all-purpose flour

¾ cup cooked wild rice

¼ cup pine nuts

¾ teaspoon celery seeds

1 teaspoon bread machine yeast

2/3 cup dried cranberries

1/8 teaspoon black pepper, ground

DIRECTIONS:

1. Add all of the ingredients to your bread machine, carefully following the instructions of the manufacturer (except cranberries).
2. Set the program of your bread machine to *Basic/White Bread* and set crust type to *Light*.
3. Press START.
4. Once the machine beeps, add cranberries.
5. Wait until the cycle completes.
6. Once the loaf is ready, take the bucket out and let the loaf cool for 5 minutes.
7. Gently shake the bucket to remove loaf.
8. Transfer to a cooling rack, slice and serve.
9. Enjoy!

NUTRITIONAL CONTENTS:

Total Carbs: 33g

Fiber: 2g

Protein: 7g

Fat: 7.8g

Calories: 225

Spice Pumpkin Bread

Yield: 1 pound loaf / 8 slices | Prep Time + Cook Time: 2 - 3 hours

Crust Type: Medium | Program: Quick Bread

- Butter for grease
- 1½ cups pumpkin puree
- 3 whole eggs
- 1/3 cup melted butter, at room temperature
- 1 cup sugar
- 3 cups all-purpose flour
- 1½ teaspoons baking powder
- ¾ teaspoon ground cinnamon
- ½ teaspoon baking soda
- ¼ teaspoon ground nutmeg
- ¼ teaspoon ground ginger
- ¼ teaspoon salt
- Pinch of ground cloves

DIRECTIONS:

1. Grease the bucket with butter.
2. Add pumpkin, eggs, butter, and sugar to the bucket.
3. Set the program of your bread machine to Quick Rapid Bread and set crust type to *Medium*.
4. Press START.
5. Take a bowl and add flour, baking powder, cinnamon, baking soda, nutmeg, ginger, salt, cloves and add the mixture to the machine once the machine beeps.
6. Wait until the cycle completes.
7. Once the loaf is ready, take the bucket out and let the loaf cool for 5 minutes.
8. Gently shake the bucket to remove loaf.
9. Transfer to a cooling rack, slice and serve.
10. Enjoy!

NUTRITIONAL CONTENTS:

Total Carbs: 43g

Fiber: 1g

Protein: 5g

Fat: 7g

Calories: 251

Lemon Flavored Poppy Loaf

Yield: 1 pound loaf / 8 slices | Prep Time + Cook Time: 3 - 4 hours

Crust Type: Light | Program: Basic/White Bread

- 1 and 1/3 cups hot water
- 3 tablespoons powdered milk
- 2 tablespoons Crisco shortening
- 2 tablespoons sugar
- 1½ teaspoon salt
- 1 tablespoon lemon juice
- 4¼ cups bread flour
- ½ teaspoon nutmeg
- 2 teaspoons grated lemon rind
- 2 tablespoons poppy seeds
- 1¼ teaspoon yeast
- 2 teaspoons wheat gluten

DIRECTIONS:

1. Add all of the ingredients to your bread machine, carefully following the instructions of the manufacturer.
2. Set the program of your bread machine to *Basic/White Bread* and set crust type to *Light*.
3. Press START.
4. Wait until the cycle completes.
5. Once the loaf is ready, take the bucket out and let the loaf cool for 5 minutes.
6. Gently shake the bucket to remove loaf.
7. Transfer to a cooling rack, slice and serve.
8. Enjoy!

NUTRITIONAL CONTENTS:

Total Carbs: 9g, Fiber: 1g, Protein: 1.6g, Fat: 3.32g, Calories: 69

Hearty Apple Pie Bread

Yield: 1 pound loaf / 8 slices | Prep Time + Cook Time: 3 hours 10 minutes

Crust Type: Medium | Program: Basic/White Bread

- 1½ teaspoons active dry yeast
- 1½ teaspoons ground cinnamon
- 3¼ cups bread flour
- 1½ teaspoons salt
- 3 tablespoons powdered buttermilk
- 1¼ cups apple pie filling
- 1½ tablespoons butter, soft
- ½ cup water

DIRECTIONS:

1. Add all of the ingredients to your bread machine, carefully following the instructions of the manufacturer.
2. Set the program of your bread machine to *Basic/White Bread* and set crust type to *Medium*.
3. Press START.
4. Wait until the cycle completes.
5. Once the loaf is ready, take the bucket out and let the loaf cool for 5 minutes.
6. Gently shake the bucket to remove loaf.
7. Transfer to a cooling rack, slice and serve.
8. Enjoy!

NUTRITIONAL CONTENTS:

Total Carbs: 35g

Fiber: 1g

Protein: 5g

Fat: 2g

Calories: 182

Hawaiian Banana Bread

Yield: 1 pound loaf / 8 slices | Prep Time + Cook Time: 3 hours 10 minutes

Crust Type: Light | Program: Basic/White Bread

½ cup mashed banana

½ cup crushed pineapple and juice

1 whole egg

¼ cup milk

¼ cup margarine, soft

½ teaspoon salt

1/3 cup white sugar

½ cup instant potato flakes

3 cups bread flour

1½ teaspoons active dry yeast

DIRECTIONS:

1. Add all of the ingredients to your bread machine, carefully following the instructions of the manufacturer.
2. Set the program of your bread machine to *Basic/White Bread* and set crust type to *Light*.
3. Press START.
4. Once the bread maker signals, add cranberries.
5. Wait until the cycle completes.
6. Once the loaf is ready, take the bucket out and let the loaf cool for 5 minutes.
7. Gently shake the bucket to remove loaf.
8. Transfer to a cooling rack, slice and serve.
9. Enjoy!

NUTRITIONAL CONTENTS:

Total Carbs: 29g

Fiber: 1g

Protein: 5g

Fat: 4g

Calories: 169

Hearty Cappuccino Orange Delight

Yield: 1 pound loaf / 8 slices | Prep Time + Cook Time: 3 hours 10 minutes

Crust Type: Medium | Program: Basic/White Bread

- 1 cup water
- 1 tablespoon instant coffee granules
- 2 tablespoons butter soft
- 1 teaspoon orange peel, grated
- 3 cups bread flour
- 2 tablespoons dry milk
- ¼ cup sugar
- 1¼ teaspoons salt
- 2¼ teaspoons bread machine yeast

DIRECTIONS:

1. Add all of the ingredients to your bread machine, carefully following the instructions of the manufacturer.
2. Set the program of your bread machine to *Basic/White Bread* and set crust type to *Medium*.
3. Press START.
4. Wait until the cycle completes.
5. Once the loaf is ready, take the bucket out and let the loaf cool for 5 minutes.
6. Gently shake the bucket to remove loaf.
7. Transfer to a cooling rack, slice and serve.
8. Enjoy!

NUTRITIONAL CONTENTS:

Total Carbs: 31g

Fiber: 1g

Protein: 4g

Fat: 3g

Calories: 155

Vegetable Bread

Healthy Celery Loaf

Yield: 1 pound loaf / 8 slices | Prep Time + Cook Time: 3 hours 10 minutes
Crust Type: Medium | Program: Basic/White Bread

1 can (10 ounces) cream of celery soup

3 tablespoons low-fat milk, heated

1 tablespoon vegetable oil

1¼ teaspoons celery salt

¾ cup celery, fresh/sliced thin

1 tablespoon celery leaves, fresh, chopped

1 whole egg

¼ teaspoon sugar

3 cups bread flour

¼ teaspoon ginger

½ cup quick-cooking oats

2 tablespoons gluten

2 teaspoons celery seeds

1 pack of active dry yeast

DIRECTIONS:

1. Add all of the ingredients to your bread machine, carefully following the instructions of the manufacturer
2. Set the program of your bread machine to Basic/White Bread and set crust type to Medium
3. Press START
4. Wait until the cycle completes
5. Once the loaf is ready, take the bucket out and let the loaf cool for 5 minutes
6. Gently shake the bucket to remove loaf
7. Transfer to a cooling rack, slice and serve
8. Enjoy!

NUTRITIONAL CONTENTS:

Total Carbs: 8g, Fiber: 1g, Protein: 3g, Fat: 4g, Calories: 73

Cheesy Broccoli & Cauliflower Health Bread

Yield: 1 pound loaf / 8 slices | Prep Time + Cook Time: 3 hours 10 minutes

Crust Type: Medium | Program: Basic/White Bread

- ¼ cup water
- 4 tablespoons olive oil
- 1 egg white
- 1 teaspoon lemon juice
- 2/3 cup grated cheddar cheese
- 3 tablespoons green onion
- ½ cup broccoli, chopped
- ½ cup cauliflower, chopped
- ½ teaspoon lemon pepper seasoning
- 2 cups bread flour
- 1 teaspoon bread machine yeast

DIRECTIONS:

1. Add all of the ingredients to your bread machine, carefully following the instructions of the manufacturer
2. Set the program of your bread machine to *Basic/White Bread* and set crust type to *Medium*
3. Press START
4. Wait until the cycle completes
5. Once the loaf is ready, take the bucket out and let the loaf cool for 5 minutes
6. Gently shake the bucket to remove loaf
7. Transfer to a cooling rack, slice and serve
8. Enjoy!

NUTRITIONAL CONTENTS:

Total Carbs: 17g

Fiber: 2g

Protein: 5g

Fat: 8g

Calories: 156

Feisty Green Onion Bread

Yield: 1 pound loaf / 8 slices | Prep Time + Cook Time: 3 hours 10 minutes

Crust Type: Medium | Program: Basic/White Bread

- ½ cup green onion, sliced
- ½ teaspoon dried basil
- ½ teaspoon dried thyme
- ¼ teaspoon dried rosemary
- 2 tablespoons butter
- 1 cup milk
- 1 whole egg
- 2 tablespoons sugar
- ¾ teaspoons salt
- 3 cups bread flour
- 2 teaspoons active dry yeast

DIRECTIONS:

1. Add all of the ingredients to your bread machine, carefully following the instructions of the manufacturer
2. Set the program of your bread machine to *Basic/White Bread* and set crust type to *Medium*
3. Press START
4. Wait until the cycle completes
5. Once the loaf is ready, take the bucket out and let the loaf cool for 5 minutes
6. Gently shake the bucket to remove loaf
7. Transfer to a cooling rack, slice and serve
8. Enjoy!

NUTRITIONAL CONTENTS:

Total Carbs: 27g

Fiber: 2g

Protein: 3g

Fat: 4g

Calories: 161

Hot Paprika Onion Bread

Yield: 1 pound loaf / 8 slices | Prep Time + Cook Time: 2 - 3 hours

Crust Type: Light | Program: Basic/White Bread

1 cup water at room temperature

2 tablespoons butter, soft

1/3 cup onion, finely chopped

1½ teaspoon salt

1 teaspoon sugar

1 teaspoon paprika

3 cups bread flour

1 pack active dry yeast

DIRECTIONS:

1. Add all of the ingredients to your bread machine, carefully following the instructions of the manufacturer
2. Set the program of your bread machine to *Basic/White Bread* and set crust type to *Light*
3. Press START
4. Wait until the cycle completes
5. Once the loaf is ready, take the bucket out and let the loaf cool for 5 minutes
6. Gently shake the bucket to remove loaf
7. Transfer to a cooling rack, slice and serve
8. Enjoy!

NUTRITIONAL CONTENTS:

Total Carbs: 17g

Fiber: 1g

Protein: 3g

Fat: 1g

Calories: 92

Caraway Potato Loaf

Yield: 1 pound loaf / 8 slices | Prep Time + Cook Time: 2 - 3 hours

Crust Type: Medium | Program: Basic/White Bread

1¼ cups water

2 tablespoons butter, at room temperature

3 cups bread flour

2 teaspoons caraway seeds

½ cup instant mashed potatoes, powdered

1 tablespoon white sugar

1½ teaspoon salt

2 teaspoons bread machine yeast

DIRECTIONS:

1. Add all of the ingredients to your bread machine, carefully following the instructions of the manufacturer
2. Set the program of your bread machine to *Basic/White Bread* and set crust type to *Medium*
3. Press START
4. Wait until the cycle completes
5. Once the loaf is ready, take the bucket out and let the loaf cool for 5 minutes
6. Gently shake the bucket to remove loaf
7. Transfer to a cooling rack, slice and serve
8. Enjoy!

NUTRITIONAL CONTENTS:

Total Carbs: 27g

Fiber: 1g

Protein: 5g

Fat: 2.3g

Calories: 203

Zucchini Herbed Bread

Yield: 1 pound loaf / 8 slices | Prep Time + Cook Time: 2 - 3 hours

Crust Type: Light | Program: Basic/White Bread

½ cup water

2 teaspoon honey

1 tablespoons oil

¾ cup zucchini, grated

¾ cup whole wheat flour

2 cups bread flour

1 tablespoon fresh basil, chopped

2 teaspoon sesame seeds

1 teaspoon salt

1½ teaspoon active dry yeast

DIRECTIONS:

1. Add all of the ingredients to your bread machine, carefully following the instructions of the manufacturer
2. Set the program of your bread machine to *Basic/White Bread* and set crust type to *Light*
3. Press START
4. Wait until the cycle completes
5. Once the loaf is ready, take the bucket out and let the loaf cool for 5 minutes
6. Gently shake the bucket to remove loaf
7. Transfer to a cooling rack, slice and serve
8. Enjoy!

NUTRITIONAL CONTENTS:

Total Carbs: 28g

Fiber: 2g

Protein: 5g

Fat: 1g

Calories: 153

Garden Variety Veggie Bread

Yield: 1 pound loaf / 8 slices | Prep Time + Cook Time: 2 - 3 hours

Crust Type: Light | Program: Basic/White Bread

½ cup warm buttermilk

3 tablespoons water, at room temperature

1 tablespoon canola oil

2/3 cup zucchini, shredded

2 tablespoons green onions, chopped

¼ cup red bell pepper, chopped

2 tablespoons Parmesan cheese, grated

2 tablespoons sugar

1 teaspoon salt

½ teaspoon lemon-pepper seasoning

½ cup old fashioned oats

2½ cups bread flour

1½ teaspoon dry yeast

DIRECTIONS:

1. Add all of the ingredients to your bread machine, carefully following the instructions of the manufacturer
2. Set the program of your bread machine to *Basic/White Bread* and set crust type to *Light*
3. Press START
4. Wait until the cycle completes
5. Once the loaf is ready, take the bucket out and let the loaf cool for 5 minutes
6. Gently shake the bucket to remove loaf
7. Transfer to a cooling rack, slice and serve
8. Enjoy!

NUTRITIONAL CONTENTS:

Total Carbs: 18g, Fiber: 1g, Protein: 4g, Fat: 1g, Calories: 94

Italian Onion Bread

Yield: 1 pound loaf / 8 slices | Prep Time + Cook Time: 3 - 4 hours

Crust Type: Light | Program: Basic/White Bread

1 cup warm milk, at room temperature

1 large whole egg

2 tablespoons butter, soft

¼ cup dried onion, minced

1½ teaspoons salt

2 tablespoons dried parsley flakes

1 teaspoon dried oregano

3½ cups bread flour

2 teaspoons dry yeast

DIRECTIONS:

1. Add all of the ingredients to your bread machine, carefully following the instructions of the manufacturer
2. Set the program of your bread machine to *Basic/White Bread* and set crust type to *Light*
3. Press START
4. Wait until the cycle completes
5. Once the loaf is ready, take the bucket out and let the loaf cool for 5 minutes
6. Gently shake the bucket to remove loaf
7. Transfer to a cooling rack, slice and serve
8. Enjoy!

NUTRITIONAL CONTENTS:

Total Carbs: 23g

Fiber: 1g

Protein: 5g

Fat: 2g

Calories: 125

Spicy Hot Red Pepper Loaf

Yield: 1 pound loaf / 8 slices | Prep Time + Cook Time: 3 hours 10 minutes

Crust Type: Medium | Program: Basic/White Bread

¾ cup + 1 tablespoons milk at room temperature

2 and 2/3 tablespoons red pepper relish

4 teaspoons chopped roasted red pepper

2 tablespoons melted butter, cooled

2 tablespoons light brown sugar

2/3 teaspoon salt

2 cups white bread flour

1 teaspoon bread machine yeast

DIRECTIONS:

1. Add all of the ingredients to your bread machine, carefully following the instructions of the manufacturer
2. Set the program of your bread machine to *Basic/White Bread* and set crust type to *Medium*
3. Press START
4. Wait until the cycle completes
5. Once the loaf is ready, take the bucket out and let the loaf cool for 5 minutes
6. Gently shake the bucket to remove loaf
7. Transfer to a cooling rack, slice and serve
8. Enjoy!

NUTRITIONAL CONTENTS:

Total Carbs: 28g

Fiber: 2g

Protein: 4g

Fat: 4g

Calories: 167

Sauerkraut Rye Bread

Yield: 1 pound loaf / 8 slices | Prep Time + Cook Time: 3 hours 10 minutes

Crust Type: Medium | Program: Basic/White Bread

1 cup sauerkraut, rinsed and drained

¾ cup warm water

1½ tablespoons molasses

1½ tablespoons butter

1½ tablespoons brown sugar

1 teaspoon caraway seeds

1½ teaspoons salt

1 cup rye flour

2 cups bread flour

1½ teaspoons active dry yeast

DIRECTIONS:

1. Add all of the ingredients to your bread machine, carefully following the instructions of the manufacturer.
2. Set the program of your bread machine to *Basic/White Bread* and set crust type to *Medium*.
3. Press START.
4. Wait until the cycle completes.
5. Once the loaf is ready, take the bucket out and let the loaf cool for 5 minutes.
6. Gently shake the bucket to remove loaf.
7. Transfer to a cooling rack, slice and serve.
8. Enjoy!

NUTRITIONAL CONTENTS:

Total Carbs: 12g

Fiber: 1g

Protein: 2g

Fat: 2g

Calories: 74

Sweet Bread

Sweet Challah

Yield: 1 pound loaf / 8 slices | Prep Time + Cook Time: 3 hours 10 minutes

Crust Type: Light | Program: Basic/White Bread

¾ cup milk

2 whole eggs

3 tablespoons margarine

3 cups bread flour

¼ cup white sugar

1½ teaspoons salt

1½ teaspoons active dry yeast

DIRECTIONS:

1. Add all of the ingredients to your bread machine, carefully following the instructions of the manufacturer
2. Set the program of your bread machine to *Basic/White Bread* and set crust type to *Light*
3. Press START
4. Wait until the cycle completes
5. Once the loaf is ready, take the bucket out and let the loaf cool for 5 minutes
6. Gently shake the bucket to remove loaf
7. Transfer to a cooling rack, slice and serve
8. Enjoy!

NUTRITIONAL CONTENTS:

Total Carbs: 30g, Fiber: 1g, Protein: 6g, Fat: 4g, Calories: 184

Sweet Sour Maple Loaf

Yield: 1 pound loaf / 8 slices | Prep Time + Cook Time: 2 - 3 hours

Crust Type: Medium | Program: Basic/White Bread

- 6 tablespoons water at 80°F
- 6 tablespoons sour cream
- 1½ tablespoons butter, at room temperature
- ¾ tablespoons maple syrup
- ½ teaspoon salt
- 1¾ cups white bread flour
- 1 and 1/8 teaspoons bread machine yeast

DIRECTIONS:

1. Add all of the ingredients to your bread machine, carefully following the instructions of the manufacturer
2. Set the program of your bread machine to *Basic/White Bread* and set crust type to *Light*
3. Press START
4. Wait until the cycle completes
5. Once the loaf is ready, take the bucket out and let the loaf cool for 5 minutes
6. Gently shake the bucket to remove loaf
7. Transfer to a cooling rack, slice and serve
8. Enjoy!

NUTRITIONAL CONTENTS:

Total Carbs: 31g

Fiber: 3g

Protein: 4g

Fat: 11g

Calories: 231

Sweet Almond Anise Bread

Yield: 1 pound loaf / 8 slices | Prep Time + Cook Time: 3 hours 10 minutes

Crust Type: Medium | Program: Basic/White Bread

¾ cup water

¼ cup butter

¼ cup sugar

½ teaspoon salt

3 cups bread flour

1 teaspoon anise seed

2 teaspoons active dry yeast

½ cup almonds, chopped

DIRECTIONS:

1. Add all of the ingredients to your bread machine, carefully following the instructions of the manufacturer (except almonds)
2. Set the program of your bread machine to *Basic/White Bread* and set crust type to *Medium*
3. Press START
4. Add almonds once the machine starts beeping
5. Wait until the cycle completes
6. Once the loaf is ready, take the bucket out and let the loaf cool for 5 minutes
7. Gently shake the bucket to remove loaf
8. Transfer to a cooling rack, slice and serve
9. Enjoy!

NUTRITIONAL CONTENTS:

Total Carbs: 7g

Fiber: 1g

Protein: 3g

Fat: 4g

Calories: 87

Choco Banana Oatmeal Loaf

Yield: 1 pound loaf / 8 slices | Prep Time + Cook Time: 2 - 3 hours

Crust Type: Medium | Program: Basic/White Bread

- 3 bananas, mashed
- 2 whole eggs, at room temperature
- ¾ cup packed light brown sugar
- 1/2 cup butter
- ½ cup sour cream
- ¼ cup sugar
- 1½ teaspoons vanilla extract
- 1 cup all-purpose flour
- ½ cup quick oats
- 2 tablespoons unsweetened cocoa powder
- 1 teaspoon baking soda

DIRECTIONS:

1. Add banana, eggs, brown sugar, butter, sour cream, vanilla and sugar to the bread machine
2. Set the program of your bread machine to Quick/Rapid Bread and set crust type to *Medium*
3. Press START
4. Mix the dry ingredients in a bowl and add the dry ingredients to the bread machine once the machine beeps
5. Wait until the cycle completes
6. Once the loaf is ready, take the bucket out and let the loaf cool for 5 minutes
7. Gently shake the bucket to remove loaf
8. Transfer to a cooling rack, slice and serve
9. Enjoy!

NUTRITIONAL CONTENTS:

Total Carbs: 31g

Fiber: 3g

Protein: 4g

Fat: 11g

Calories: 231

Honeylicious Loaf

Yield: 1 pound loaf / 8 slices | Prep Time + Cook Time: 3 hours 10 minutes

Crust Type: Medium | Program: Basic/White Bread

¾ cups milk, at 80°F

2 tablespoons honey

1 tablespoon butter, melted and cooled

¾ teaspoon salt

½ cup whole wheat flour

½ cup prepared granola crushed

1¼ cups white bread flour

1 teaspoon bread machine yeast

DIRECTIONS:

1. Add all of the ingredients to your bread machine, carefully following the instructions of the manufacturer
2. Set the program of your bread machine to *Basic/White Bread* and set crust type to *Medium*
3. Press START
4. Wait until the cycle completes
5. Once the loaf is ready, take the bucket out and let the loaf cool for 5 minutes
6. Gently shake the bucket to remove loaf
7. Transfer to a cooling rack, slice and serve
8. Enjoy!

NUTRITIONAL CONTENTS:

Total Carbs: 33g

Fiber: 1g

Protein: 6g

Fat: 5g

Calories: 151

Healthy Sweet Flaxseed Loaf

Yield: 1 pound loaf / 8 slices | Prep Time + Cook Time: 2 - 3 hours

Crust Type: Medium | Program: Basic/White Bread

- ¾ cup milk, at room temperature
- 1 tablespoon melted butter
- 1 tablespoon honey
- ¾ teaspoon salt
- 2 tablespoons flaxseeds
- 2 cups white bread flour
- ¾ teaspoon bread machine yeast

DIRECTIONS:

1. Add all of the ingredients to your bread machine, carefully following the instructions of the manufacturer
2. Set the program of your bread machine to *Basic/White Bread* and set crust type to *Medium*
3. Press START
4. Wait until the cycle completes
5. Once the loaf is ready, take the bucket out and let the loaf cool for 5 minutes
6. Gently shake the bucket to remove loaf
7. Transfer to a cooling rack, slice and serve
8. Enjoy!

NUTRITIONAL CONTENTS:

Total Carbs: 28g

Fiber: 1g

Protein: 6g

Fat: 3g

Calories: 158

Crunchy Sweet Raisin Loaf

Yield: 1 pound loaf / 8 slices | Prep Time + Cook Time: 3 hours 10 minutes

Crust Type: Medium | Program: Basic/White Bread

- 1/3 cup milk, at 80°F
- 2 whole eggs, at room temperature
- 4 teaspoons butter, melted and cooled
- 2 and 2/3 tablespoons sugar
- 2/3 teaspoons salt
- 1 and 1/3 teaspoons lemon zest
- 2 cups white bread flour
- 1 and 1/3 teaspoons bread machine yeast
- ¼ cup slivered almonds
- ¼ cup golden raisins

DIRECTIONS:

1. Add all of the ingredients to your bread machine, carefully following the instructions of the manufacturer (except almonds and raisins)
2. Set the program of your bread machine to *Basic/White Bread* and set crust type to *Medium*
3. Press START
4. Once the machine signals, add nuts and raisins
5. Wait until the cycle completes
6. Once the loaf is ready, take the bucket out and let the loaf cool for 5 minutes
7. Gently shake the bucket to remove loaf
8. Transfer to a cooling rack, slice and serve
9. Enjoy!

NUTRITIONAL CONTENTS:

Total Carbs: 33g

Fiber: 1g

Protein: 6g

Fat: 5g

Calories: 195

Hazelnut Honey Loaf

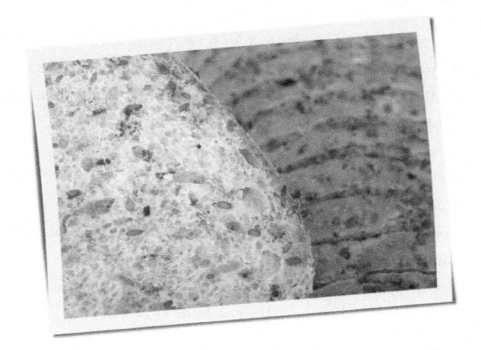

Yield: 1 pound loaf / 8 slices | Prep Time + Cook Time: 3 hours 10 minutes

Crust Type: Medium | Program: Basic/White Bread

½ cup milk, at room temperature

2 teaspoons melted butter, cooled

2 teaspoons honey

2/3 teaspoons salt

1/3 cup cooked wild rice, cooled

1/3 cup whole wheat flour

2/3 teaspoons caraway seeds

1 cup + 1 tablespoon white bread flour

1 teaspoon bread machine yeast

1/3 cup hazelnuts, chopped

DIRECTIONS:

1. Add all of the ingredients to your bread machine, carefully following the instructions of the manufacturer
2. Set the program of your bread machine to *Basic/White Bread* and set crust type to *Medium*
3. Press START
4. Wait until the cycle completes
5. Once the loaf is ready, take the bucket out and let the loaf cool for 5 minutes
6. Gently shake the bucket to remove loaf
7. Transfer to a cooling rack, slice and serve
8. Enjoy!

NUTRITIONAL CONTENTS:

Total Carbs: 23g

Fiber: 1g

Protein: 4g

Fat: 4g

Calories: 140

Multi-Grain Honey Bread

Yield: 1 pound loaf / 8 slices | Prep Time + Cook Time: 2 - 3 hours

Crust Type: Medium | Program: Basic/White Bread

1 and 1/3 cups warm water

1 tablespoon active dry yeast

3 tablespoons dry milk powder

2 tablespoons honey

2 teaspoons salt

1 whole egg

1 cup whole wheat flour

2½ cups bread flour

¾ cups 7-grain cereal

DIRECTIONS:

1. Add all of the ingredients to your bread machine, carefully following the instructions of the manufacturer
2. Set the program of your bread machine to *Basic/White Bread* and set crust type to *Medium*
3. Press START
4. Wait until the cycle completes
5. Once the loaf is ready, take the bucket out and let the loaf cool for 5 minutes
6. Gently shake the bucket to remove loaf
7. Transfer to a cooling rack, slice and serve
8. Enjoy!

NUTRITIONAL CONTENTS:

Total Carbs: 50g

Fiber: 1g

Protein: 10g

Fat: 6g

Calories: 47

Holiday Bread

Christmas Eggnog Bread

Yield: 1 pound loaf / 8 slices | Prep Time + Cook Time: 3 hours 10 minutes

Crust Type: Light | Program: Basic/White Bread

- 1 cup eggnog
- ½ cup milk
- 4 cups bread flour
- ½ cup dried cranberries
- 1¼ teaspoons salt
- 2 tablespoons sugar
- 1 tablespoon butter
- 1 teaspoon cinnamon
- 1¾ teaspoons yeast

DIRECTIONS:

1. Add all of the ingredients to your bread machine, carefully following the instructions of the manufacturer
2. Set the program of your bread machine to *Basic/White Bread* and set crust type to *Light*
3. Press START
4. Wait until the cycle completes
5. Once the loaf is ready, take the bucket out and let the loaf cool for 5 minutes
6. Gently shake the bucket to remove loaf
7. Transfer to a cooling rack, slice and serve
8. Enjoy!

NUTRITIONAL CONTENTS:

Total Carbs: 11g, Fiber: 1g, Protein: 2.5g, Fat: 3g, Calories: 77

St. Patrick's Rum Bread

Yield: 1 pound loaf / 8 slices | Prep Time + Cook Time: 3 hours 40 minutes

Crust Type: Medium | Program: Basic/White Bread

- 1 whole egg
- 1 tablespoon rum extract
- 3 tablespoons bread flour
- 3 tablespoons packed brown sugar
- 1¼ teaspoons salt
- ½ teaspoon ground cinnamon
- ¼ teaspoon ground nutmeg
- ¼ teaspoon ground cardamom
- 1 teaspoon bread machine yeast

TOPPING

1 egg yolk, beaten

1½ teaspoon brown sugar

1½ teaspoon pecans, chopped

DIRECTIONS:

1. Break an egg into 1 cup and add water to fill out a measuring cup
2. Add egg mixture to the machine
3. Add all of the ingredients to your bread machine, carefully following the instructions of the manufacturer
4. Set the program of your bread machine to *Basic/White Bread* and set crust type to *Medium*
5. Press START
6. When just 40 minutes of the cycle remains, make the topping mixture and brush the top of the bread
7. Wait until the cycle completes
8. Once the loaf is ready, take the bucket out and let the loaf cool for 5 minutes
9. Gently shake the bucket to remove loaf
10. Transfer to a cooling rack, slice and serve
11. Enjoy!

NUTRITIONAL CONTENTS:

Total Carbs: 31g, Fiber: 1g, Protein: 4g, Fat: 4g, Calories: 170

White Chocolate Cranberry Party Loaf

Yield: 1 pound loaf / 8 slices | Prep Time + Cook Time: 3 hours 40 minutes

Crust Type: Medium | Program: Basic/White Bread

½ cup milk, at room temperature

1 egg, at room temperature

2/3 teaspoons pure vanilla extract

4 teaspoons sugar

½ teaspoon salt

2 cups white bread flour

¾ teaspoon instant yeast

½ cup white chocolate chips

½ cup cranberries

DIRECTIONS:

1. Add all of the ingredients to your bread machine, carefully following the instructions of the manufacturer (except chocolate chips and cranberries)
2. Set the program of your bread machine to *Basic/White Bread* and set crust type to *Light*
3. Press START
4. Add chocolate chips and cranberries once the machine beeps
5. Wait until the cycle completes
6. Once the loaf is ready, take the bucket out and let the loaf cool for 5 minutes
7. Gently shake the bucket to remove loaf
8. Transfer to a cooling rack, slice and serve

NUTRITIONAL CONTENTS:

Total Carbs: 34g, Fiber: 1g, Protein: 5g, Fat: 5g, Calories: 201

Portuguese Holiday Loaf

Yield: 1 pound loaf / 8 slices | Prep Time + Cook Time: 2 - 3 hours

Crust Type: Light | Program: Sweet Bread

2/3 cup milk at 80°F

1 whole egg, at room temperature

4 teaspoons butter, soft

1/3 cup sugar

2 cups white bread flour

1½ teaspoons bread machine instant

DIRECTIONS:

1. Add all of the ingredients to your bread machine, carefully following the instructions of the manufacturer
2. Set the program of your bread machine to Sweet Bread and set crust type to *Light*
3. Press START
4. Wait until the cycle completes
5. Once the loaf is ready, take the bucket out and let the loaf cool for 5 minutes
6. Gently shake the bucket to remove loaf
7. Transfer to a cooling rack, slice and serve
8. Enjoy!

NUTRITIONAL CONTENTS:

Total Carbs: 34g

Fiber: 1g

Protein: 5g

Fat: 3g

Calories: 180

Grandma's Favorite Gingerbread

Yield: 1 pound loaf / 8 slices | Prep Time + Cook Time: 2 - 3 hours

Crust Type: Medium | Program: Sweet Bread

- 2/3 cup buttermilk at 80°F
- 1 egg, at room temperature
- 2 and 2/3 tablespoons dark molasses
- 2 teaspoons melted butter, cooled
- 2 tablespoons sugar
- 1 teaspoon salt
- 1 teaspoon ground ginger
- 2/3 teaspoon ground cinnamon
- 1/3 teaspoon ground nutmeg
- 1/8 teaspoon ground cloves
- 2 and 1/3 cups white bread flour
- 1 and 1/3 teaspoons bread machine yeast

DIRECTIONS:

1. Add all of the ingredients to your bread machine, carefully following the instructions of the manufacturer
2. Set the program of your bread machine to Sweet Bread and set crust type to *Medium*
3. Press START
4. Wait until the cycle completes
5. Once the loaf is ready, take the bucket out and let the loaf cool for 5 minutes
6. Gently shake the bucket to remove loaf
7. Transfer to a cooling rack, slice and serve
8. Enjoy!

NUTRITIONAL CONTENTS:

Total Carbs: 38g

Fiber: 1g

Protein: 5g

Fat: 2g

Calories: 190

Kitchen Tools

Kitchen Scale

A kitchen scale is a must-have kitchen tool. Preparing certain types of food without one is practically impossible. Yes, there are cups, but when it comes to dough-based meals, a kitchen scale is a necessary equipment. The best example is a bread, which is hard to make without a kitchen scale. The reason behind it is **because flour is a compressible, and measurement in cups will sometimes just not be accurate**. To get your bread dough perfect, we suggest you use kitchen scales. You can find classic and digital ones, but for the best accuracy, choose digital scales. They are so much easier to use, plus most of them have very modern and interesting designs.

Pastry Brush

Basting brush or pastry brush looks similar to a paintbrush. It is made of nylon or plastic fiber. It is used to spread glaze, oil or butter on food.

Cheese Grater

Pizza is a delicious dish, and we all would agree it would not be the same without cheese on it. Cheese is a staple ingredient for pizza making, and when speaking about the cheese, it cannot be used in large slices on the pizza. **To get your cheese perfectly grated, use stainless-steel cheese graters.** They will perfectly grate the cheese and make it properly prepared for use on pizza. Besides grating the cheese, you can grate some other ingredients as well, like salami or bell peppers.

Cooking Measurement Conversion

US Dry Measurements

1/16 teaspoon	a dash
1/8 teaspoon	a pinch
3 teaspoons	1 tablespoon
¼ cup	4 tablespoons
1/3 cup	5 tablespoons + 1 teaspoon
½ cup	8 tablespoons
¾ cup	12 tablespoons
1 cup	16 tablespoons
1 pound	16 ounces

US Liquid Volume Measurements

8 fluid ounces	1 cup
1 pint = 2 cups	16 fluid ounces
1 quart = 2 pints	4 cups
1 gallon = 4 quarts	16 cups

Grocery Shopping List

GRAINS & FLOURS

- [ ] Wheat Flour
- [ ] Semolina
- [ ] Corn Flour
- [ ] Bread Flour
- [ ] Wholemeal Flour
- [ ] Whole-grain Flour
- [ ] Rye Flour
- [ ] Rice
- [ ] Oatmeal
- [ ] Granola
- [ ] 7-grain cereal
- [ ] Potato Flakes
- [ ] Apple Pie Filling
- [ ] Bran
- [ ] Milk Powder
- [ ] Yeast
- [ ] Gluten

SEASONINGS

- [ ] Sugar
- [ ] Salt
- [ ] Vanilla
- [ ] Paprika
- [ ] Cumin
- [ ] Rosemary
- [ ] Basil
- [ ] Italian Herbs
- [ ] Parsley
- [ ] Lavender
- [ ] Thyme
- [ ] Cinnamon
- [ ] Nutmeg
- [ ] Oregano
- [ ] Saffron
- [ ] Turmeric
- [ ] Cardamon
- [ ] Horseradish
- [ ] Pepper
- [ ] Lemon Pepper
- [ ] Cloves

DAIRY

- Milk
- Sour Cream
- Butter
- Whey
- Buttermilk
- Crisco Shortening
- Margarine
- Sunflower Milk
- Cream Cheese
- Mozzarella
- Cottage Cheese
- Ricotta
- Cheddar
- Parmesan
- Monterey Jack
- Blue Cheese

NUTS AND SEEDS

- Eggs
- Poppy Seeds
- Almond
- Peanuts
- Caraway Seeds
- Sesame Seeds
- Walnut
- Pistachios
- Pecans
- Anise Seeds
- Pine Nuts
- Celery Seeds
- Flaxseeds
- Hazelnuts

OILS, VINEGAR, & CONDIMENTS

- Olive Oil
- Almond Oil
- Sunflower Oil
- Corn Oil
- Mustard
- Vegetable Oil
- Canola Oil

DRIED HERBS, VEGETABLES & SPICES

- Italian Herbs
- Dried Onion
- Dried Fruits
- Sun-dried Tomatoes
- Ginger
- Garlic

BEVERAGES

- [ ] Light Beer
- [ ] Brewed Coffee
- [ ] Olive Brine
- [ ] Lemon Juice
- [ ] Eggnog
- [ ] Rum Extract
- [ ] Coffee Granules

SWEETS

- [ ] Honey
- [ ] Maple Syrup
- [ ] Raisings
- [ ] Candied Fruits
- [ ] Dried Cranberries
- [ ] Cocoa Powder
- [ ] Chocolate Chips
- [ ] Molasses

FRUITS

- [ ] Apple
- [ ] Cranberry
- [ ] Orange
- [ ] Lemon
- [ ] Banana
- [ ] Pineapple

VEGETABLES

- [ ] Potato
- [ ] Chives
- [ ] Red Pepper
- [ ] Jalapeno Pepper
- [ ] Pumpkin
- [ ] Celery
- [ ] Broccoli
- [ ] Cauliflower
- [ ] Green Onion
- [ ] Onion
- [ ] Zucchini
- [ ] Bell Pepper

CANNED GOODS

- [ ] Pears
- [ ] Cream Celery Soup
- [ ] Olives
- [ ] Pimiento Olives

MEAT

- [ ] Salami

From the Author

I am a **professional chef**, and I have a big, friendly family. I **enjoy cooking at home** and pleasing my kids and wife with delicious and exceptional dishes.

And with a **bread machine**, it enables me to put a fresh loaf on our table every day. I just put various ingredients in the device and press one button. And in two hours, the house is filled with an incredible fragrance. **No smell can compare to the odor of freshly baked bread.**

We make sandwiches with bread, toast it, smear it with jam or butter, along with hundreds more ways to enjoy this salivating treat. And often, we invite friends to join us. The smell of bread always makes you feel at home.

Our Recommendations

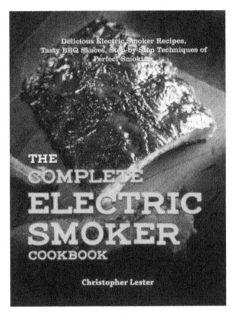

THE COMPLETE ELECTRIC SMOKER COOKBOOK is an exhaustive guide to using your electric smoker effectively.

The **DUTCH OVEN COOKBOOK** is your best guide to no-fuss cooking in just one pot.

Recipe Index

A

All-Purpose White Bread 17
Awesome Golden Corn Bread 75
Awesome Multigrain Bread 99
Awesome Rosemary Bread 47

B

Blue Cheese & Onion Loaf 124
Bran Packed Healthy Bread 91
Brazilian Nuts & Nutmeg Loaf 109

C

Caramel Apple Pecan Loaf 95
Caraway Potato Loaf 154
Cheddar Packed Olive Loaf 117
Cheese Bread 113
Cheese Grater 194
Cheesy Basil Loaf 119
Cheesy Broccoli & Cauliflower Health Bread 148
Choco Banana Oatmeal Loaf 172
Christmas Eggnog Bread 184
Cinnamon & Dried Fruits Bread 53
Cinnamon-Flavored Raisin Bread 69
Cooking Measurement Conversion 195
Cool Pumpernickel Bread 39
Corn, Poppy Seeds & Sour Cream Bread 83
Cracked Wheat Bread 79
Crispy French Bread Delight 29
Crunchy Sweet Raisin Loaf 178
Crunchy Wheat Herbed Bread 103
Cumin Tossed Fancy Bread 59

D

Delicious Flax Honey Loaf 107
Delicious Honey Lavender Bread 63
Delicious Italian Bread 33
Delicious Rice Bread 101
Double Cheese Overload 115

E

Energizing Anise Lemon Bread 67
Exuberant Egg Bread 37

F

Faithful Italian Semolina Bread 21
Feisty Green Onion Bread 150

Fragrant Cardamom Bread 73
From the Author 200
Fruit Bread 130
Fruity French Bread 130

G

Garden Variety Veggie Bread 158
Garlic & Parmesan Delight 122
Ginger Bread & Oatmeal Medley 45
Grain, Seed & Nut Bread 75
Grandma's Favorite Gingerbread 191
Great British Muffin Bread 23
Grocery Shopping List 196

H

Hawaiian Banana Bread 142
Hazelnut Honey Loaf 180
Healthy Celery Loaf 146
Healthy Sweet Flaxseed Loaf 176
Hearty Apple Pie Bread 140
Hearty Cappuccino Orange Delight 144
Hearty Oatmeal Loaf 77
Herb Garlic Cream Cheese Loaf 126
Herbal Garlic Cream Cheese Delight 55
Herbed Sausage Bread 43
Holiday Bread 184
Honey-Flavored Bread 27
Honeylicious Loaf 174

Hot Paprika Onion Bread 152
How to bake bread correctly in a bread maker? 14
How to make bread tastier and more useful? 15

I

Inspiring Cinnamon Bread 65
Irish Beer Bread 35
Italian Onion Bread 160

K

Kitchen Scale 193
Kitchen Tools 193

L

Lemon Flavored Poppy Loaf 138
Lovely Aromatic Lavender Bread 51

M

Mesmerizing Walnut Bread 89
Monterey Jack Loaf 121
Moza Salami Loaf 128
Multi-Grain Honey Bread 182
Multi-Purpose Seven Grain Bread 111
Mustard-Flavored General Bread 19

O

Orange Almond Loaf 81

Orange Walnut Candied Loaf 93

Oregano Mozza-Cheese Bread 57

Original Italian Herb Bread 49

Our Recommendations 201

P

Pastry Brush 194

Pistachio Horseradish Apple Bread 87

Portuguese Holiday Loaf 189

Potato Rosemary Loaf 61

R

Ricotta & Chive Loaf 113

S

Sauerkraut Rye Bread 164

Sesame Seeds & Onion Bread 97

Simple Dark Rye Loaf 85

So, let's get started… 11

Spice & Herb Bread 47

Spice Pumpkin Bread 136

Spicy Hawaiian Loaf 41

Spicy Hot Red Pepper Loaf 162

St. Patrick's Rum Bread 186

Succulent Cranberry Cinnamon Loaf 132

Sunflower Seeds & Oatmeal Bread 105

Sweet Almond Anise Bread 170

Sweet Bread 166

Sweet Challah 166

Sweet Molasses Wheat Bread 25

Sweet Sour Maple Loaf 168

T

Toasty Paprika Bread 31

Traditional Bread 17

Turmeric Raisin Saffron Loaf 71

V

Vegetable Bread 146

W

White Chocolate Cranberry Party Loaf 188

Wild Rice Cranberry Delight 134

Z

Zucchini Herbed Bread 156

If you have a free minute, please leave your review of the book. Your feedback is very important for us, as well as for other readers.

https://www.amazon.com/dp/B07J4VBDNQ#customerReviews

Copyright

ALL ©COPYRIGHTS RESERVED 2018 by Christopher Lester

All Rights Reserved. No part of this publication or the information in it may be quoted from or reproduced in any form by means such as printing, scanning, photocopying or otherwise without prior written permission of the copyright holder.

Disclaimer and Terms of Use: Effort has been made to ensure that the information in this book is accurate and complete; however, the author and the publisher do not warrant the accuracy of the information, text, or graphics contained within the book due to the rapidly changing nature of science, research, known and unknown facts, and the internet. The author and the publisher do not hold any responsibility for errors, omissions, or contrary interpretation of the subject matter herein. This book is presented solely for motivational and informational purposes only

Made in the USA
Middletown, DE
02 December 2018